Marek J. Muraw

Dornier
Do 17/Do 215

KAGERO

MORE FROM KAGERO

Dornier Do 17/Do 215 • Marek J. Murawski • First edition • LUBLIN 2015

© All rights reserved. With the exception of quoting brief passages for the purposes of review, no part of this publication may be reproduced without prior written permission from the Publisher. Nazwa serii zastrzeżona w UP RP • ISBN 978-83-64596-33-9

Editing: **Marek J. Murawski** • Translation: **Tomasz Szlagor, Jarosław Dobrzyński** • Cover artwork and color profiles: **Arkadiusz Wróbel**
• Drawings: **Mariusz Łukasik** • Photos: **Dornier GmbH, via E. Kocent-Zieliński, via Marek J. Murawski, via L. Kosiński, via K. Cieślak, archiwum Kagero**
• Design: KAGERO STUDIO, Łukasz Maj

Oficyna Wydawnicza KAGERO
Akacjowa 100, Turka, os. Borek, 20-258 Lublin 62, Poland, phone/fax: (+48) 81 501 21 05
www.kagero.pl • e-mail: kagero@kagero.pl, marketing@kagero.pl
w w w . k a g e r o . p l
Distribution: **Oficyna Wydawnicza KAGERO**

My order reads: 'Reconnoitre area of Brest-Litovsk – Równe – Sarny – Bielsk, with the emphasis on airfields and railway traffic'. This was to be the first reconnaissance mission behind enemy lines our Staffel was asked to perform.

As we were getting ready, the other crews gathered around us. The day dawned murky, and the hills surrounding Allenstein (Olsztyn) were shrouded by a veil of grey haze.

"If I were you, I would stick to the railway line", said Junghaus. "You won't get lost."

"Well, I'd take along a phrase book, just in case", advised Niebelschütz. "There are few road signs in Poland, though you could always ask people working in the fields which way to go."

"Or a policeman!" laughed Klimmer.

Poor chaps! Surely their witty remarks were tainted with envy.

"We'll do fine, gentlemen", I assured them. "When we get back, I'll be counting on you to help me interpret the photos."

As our engines revved up the din drowned the hubbub of their excited voices. I tightened my parachute harness and climbed aboard the aircraft. My crew, Uffz. Kieler and Maiwald, were already inside. I turned around, waved farewell to our comrades and shouted: "I'll bring you some postcards!" Then the wheel chocks were pulled away and our machine surged forward across the field.

We orbited over the airfield and then began to climb ever higher, finally disappearing into the solid overcast clouds, which extended south as far as the eye could see. We broke clear of the clouds at 1,200 meters, and pressed on with the crystal clear, blue dome overhead. Once at 3,000 meters, we turned south, towards the border.

We carefully timed our approach. Twenty minutes later we were supposed to cross the border. It was a thrilling sensation. Down below, hidden under the layer of billowing clouds – which now, illuminated by the sun, resembled a frozen lake surface – lay enemy country. Like a seabed infested with hostile, dangerous creatures. It was time to have a look around. I motioned to the pilot. Kieler nodded in reply and down we went, submerging in the clouds. As we broke clear, I saw flat countryside spreading ahead of us. It was tinged dark brown, with patches of violet, where the heather bloomed. A wide, winding river, and a bridge in the distance.

"That's the Bug river!" yelled Kieler.

We were flying at 800 meters. I saw flashes below, next to the bridge. Bright, red balls were heading our way. They drifted slowly through the air; I had no problem tracking their advance. They looked like a string of red mice, each with a long, fiery tail – Polish anti-aircraft batteries had opened up!

I could see we were being bracketed. Those red balls were getting too close for comfort. I pointed my finger skywards. Kieler pulled up the nose of our machine and we ducked into the clouds, continuing on instruments.

One of prototypes of the reconnaissance version Dornier Do 17R, powered by Daimler Benz DB 601 B inline engines.

Pilot's position in the Do 17P, note the lack of the control yoke. MG 15 gun mount is installed in the starboard window.

So this was our baptism of fire. In fact, quite anticlimactic. I had expected it to be much more dramatic. We flew on, suspended in the opaque, milky void. One could barely see the palm of an extended hand. We had to rely exclusively on the readings of our instruments: artificial horizon, turn and bank indicator, and the clock. If our timing was right, we were over Brest-Litovsk. Again we dropped below the cloud deck. Indeed, I could recognize the distinctive, angled contours of the Brest fortress – a grey-coloured patch, clearly outlined against a brown background. We had ventured too far out to the east and now we had to turn west to take photos of an airfield.

Directly below us, the Bug river leisurely wound its way. I could see sandy shallows under the surface of the clear water. Forlorn and distant, they made me think of the moon's landscape. Suddenly... red bursts of anti-aircraft shells... At least three Flak cannons were taking pot shots at us. I motioned my hand to direct Kieler's attention to the nearby airfield. However, he made a far too wide an orbit, perhaps due to a strong head wind, and we strayed to one side of the airfield. In order to take good photographs we had to line up the target and follow a straight course for several hundred meters.

A reconnaissance Dornier Do 17 P-1 (W.Nr. 4086) of 3.(F)/Aufkl.Gr. 31 subordinated to Armeegruppe Süd; Poland, September 1939.

Do 17 P-1 of 3./Aufkl.
Gr. 10 'Tannenberg'
(a reconnaissance unit)
camouflaged at a forward
landing ground during
campaign in Poland in
September 1939.

BMW 132 engine check in
Do 17 P-1 of 3.(F)/Aufkl.Gr. 10.

Dornier Do 17 P-1
of 3.(F)/Aufkl. Gr. 11
readied for a sortie.

Dornier Do 17 V1's fuselage mock-up at Dornier's plant.

Do 17 V1 first prototype in Dornier's assembly hall.

"Man, you can do better than that!" I exclaimed.

Finally on our third pass we got it right. The aerodrome was dead ahead. In the meantime, the number of Flak bursts had increased alarmingly. The shells zoomed up, reached the highest point of their trajectory, exploded in a fiery flash and cascaded down. Most of them went off below, but some burst on either side or ahead of us. This time I had a splendid view of the airfield. As soon as I took the photos, we gunned the engines and, dodging the Flak, sped off to the south. Curiously, not a single shell fragment hit us, and no fighter scrambled to intercept us.

The farther we flew on the southerly course, the lighter the sky grew. Solid overcast gave way to broken clouds, and in the breaks we could see stretches of land merrily illuminated by the sunrays. We enjoyed the bucolic scenes below: meadows with large flocks of wild geese grazing on them, peasants toiling in the fields, and dark patches of woodland veiled in mists. From time to time we caught a glimpse of hamlets, their cottages with thatched roofs blurring into the surrounding countryside. We spotted the Kovel

Dornier Do 17 fitted with
a single tailfin was first flown
on 23rd November 1934.

railway station, clogged with trains, then passed over Równe and Sarny. Directly behind Sarny lay the Rokitna marshes – a grey, soggy wasteland mottled with white-trunked birches and pools of water. Lying prone, I marked all our findings on the map. Just then the pilot leaned to me and shouted to my ear: "Fighters on our tail!"

Simultaneously, the machine gun manned by our radio operator began to clatter. I clambered back to my station and looked behind. Indeed, three Polish PZL 24 fighters boring in on us![1] With their slim fuselages and short, stubby wings they looked very much like agitated hornets. One of them closed the distance to some

400 meters and fired its guns. Strings of white tracers groped towards us. Then the sickening noise of bullets tearing into our machine... and again... time after time. Splinters swished inside the crew compartment. Maiwald, our radio operator, curled up. A stray bullet had torn one of his trouser legs, nicked his calf and embedded itself in the cockpit roof.

One more burst of gunfire found its mark... This time our control surfaces were hit. So this was the real baptism of fire! What a nasty feeling – three against one, and we were just a hapless, hard-working 'bee' on a reconnaissance mission! If only we could turn around and

The mockup of Do 17V1 fuselage after assembly.

Associates of Professor Dornier. Sitting from left to right are Ing. Kohler, Dr Ing. Schmidt, Dr Ing. Stiess.

Dornier Do 17 V2 was passed to the Lufthansa, where it received a civil registration code D-AHAK and was named 'Rhein'.

return fire… But our task was to reconnoiter at all costs, not to fight.

Maiwald kept shooting back, whilst Kieler directed our machine into a cumulus cloud, which glided majestically across the blue sky like a white ark. We plunged inside, changed course several times, and popped out on the other side of the cloud. Almost instantly hard, metallic cracks reverberated in the cockpit. One of the Poles had tagged onto our tail and was spraying us with bullets. He was a mere 200 meters away. I felt a surge of fury overcome me. I went towards the rear, pushed Mailwald aside, and grabbed his machine gun. In the meantime Kieler accelerated into a dive, racing for the cloud layer billowing to the north of us. The Polish fighter fell behind and after a few tense moments we were again enveloped by clouds.

Half an hour had passed before we emerged into the clear. We were alone. We took up a north – north-west heading, straight towards our home base. On the way we spotted a freight train moving along the Warsaw-Białystok line. With the adrenaline still pumping through our veins from the recent scrap with fighters, we did not

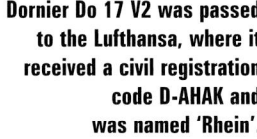

hesitate for long. For only a brief moment did the recollection of Hptm. Kerber's stern words pass through my mind: 'Avoid combat at all costs. Delivering the results of your reconnaissance run is of the utmost importance'. But now it was too late. We were racing down, and taking aim at the locomotive. Our forward-pointing gun ripped out a short burst and a geyser of steam shot up from the punctured boiler. The train slowly ground to a halt. We veered around and rushed back, going flat out 'on the deck'. We were in fact flying so low that I could see treetops bowing under the pressure of our slipstream. We made a second firing pass at the locomotive. Ahead, there was a seemingly endless column of box cars. Several people, apparently brakemen, fled in panic across the fields and away from the train. At the head of the train one man, the engine driver, could be seen. A small, black figure, aiming a rifle at us.

Again our slugs thudded into the bulky, shiny boiler. Suddenly I heard a cracking noise behind my back. Turning around, I saw a hole in my observer's seat, left by a bullet that had gone right through it to stick in the cockpit roof. The guy with the rifle was a sharp shooter, and a lucky one, too. Had I been in my seat, that bullet would have killed me. One more pass. Incredibly, the guy was still there, standing fast in his bluish, sooty overalls. With the butt of his rifle pressed to his shoulder, he drew a bead on us. For a moment a felt a sense of respect for this tough, selfless man, who dared to duel with our overwhelming firepower. However, his locomotive was already knocked out for good. As we pulled up, it was standing there, like a mortally wounded animal, its boiler bleeding off steam from numerous punctures.

At noon we landed at our airfield. We had been in the air for six hours and ten minutes. Our comrades came running up to greet us and tightly circled our machine. They counted nine

Dornier Do 17 V3 (D-ABIH) was fitted with a KLs/A17 flexible mount for 20 mm Borsig LB 204 cannon.

Dornier Do 17 V4 (D-AGYA) just like V3 served as a testbed for onboard armament of machines guns and a 20 mm cannon.

Dornier Do 17 V7, W.Nr. 657 (D-AQYK), which prototyped the E-2 variant.

bullet holes in the aircraft. We jumped to the ground in high spirits. Everybody asked questions and cheered as if we had returned from the dead. Only the officer responsible for our onboard photographic equipment remained calm. "I hope you bunch of heroes didn't let my camera get shot to pieces?" he said wryly.[2]

Design and Development

The Dornier Do 17 was designed and built in the Dornier Werke GmbH plant located in Friedrichshafen on the Bodensee (Lake Constance). The company was founded and owned by one of the most renowned German aviation designers, Prof. Claudius Dornier. He was born on 14th May 1884 at Kempten im Allgäu. The son of a French wine importer and his German wife, Claude Dornier was born and grew up in Bavaria. In 1907 he graduated from the *Technische Hochschule* (Technical University) at Munich,

where he had studied *Maschinenbau* (mechanical engineering). As a young engineer he first worked for a company designing and building steel road and rail bridges. In 1910, he joined the *Versuchsanstalt des Zeppelin-Luftschiffbaues*, an experimental facility in Friedrichshafen, which constructed airships. There he dealt with the statics and aerodynamics of airships, refined the construction of airscrews and worked on an advanced, mobile hangar for airships. Shortly before the outbreak of the First World War Dornier designed a massive airship (gas capacity of 80,000 cubic metres) for transatlantic communication. When the war broke out, there was no longer a need for an airship line to the United States of America, and the order was duly cancelled. To compensate for it, Dornier received an offer to design a large, multi-engine flying boat for military use.

While designing his flying boat, Dornier relied heavily on steel and duralumin, which made him one of the pioneers of all-metal aircraft

construction. His project was designated Rs I. The first prototype was ready in October 1915, but its further development was discontinued before it had a chance to take to the air. It was followed by Rs II, Rs III and Rs IV, which were test-flown. Besides their all-metal construction, Dornier's flying boats featured engines placed in tandem. This solution was first introduced in the Rs II, due to the lack of more powerful engines. It proved its worth, and was successfully used in many subsequent flying boat designs.

Another novelty was the boat's high-wing configuration with two fuselage-mounted sponsons to improve water stability during start and landing. In 1916 the Zeppelin Werke GmbH plant run by Dornier moved from Seemoos to Lindau-Reutin. There, in 1918, the D I single-seat, all metal fighter aircraft was prototyped, but never made it to series production.

After the armistice had been proclaimed in November 1918, Dornier continued to work in the Zeppelin Werke GmbH at Lindau-Reutin, as

Dornier Do 17 V8, W.Nr. 658, prototyped the reconnaissance version designated F-1.

Dornier Do 17 E-1's fuselage being assembled.

Fuselages of Do 17 E-1s at Dornier's assembly hall.

well as in the Flugzeugbau Friedrichshafen GmbH in Manzell. In the latter location 20 Zeppelin C II bi-plane observation aircraft were built, of which 19 were delivered to Switzerland.

Since the war was over, Dornier focused on civilian designs. On 31st July 1919, Dornier's new flying boat, designated Gs I, with a capacity of six passengers, made its maiden flight. The first air tests revealed its great potential, and the aircraft was publicly demonstrated in the Netherlands. However, the Allied Armistice Committee promptly categorized it as a type of aircraft banned by the Treaty of Versailles and ordered the prototype to be destroyed. Furthermore, Dornier was obliged to discontinue his work on two prototypes of the Gs II flying boat (with a capacity of nine passengers). Watched closely by the Allied Armistice Committee, Dornier strove to design aircraft within the limits imposed on the German aviation industry. One of them was the Cs II Delphin flying boat with a capacity of five passengers, first flown on 24th November 1920. It was followed by its land-based counterpart the C III Komet, completed the next year, and the Libelle I (Dragonfly) open-cockpit, parasol wing, monoplane flying boat.

In 1922 Zeppelin Werke GmbH at Lindau-Reutin was re-named Dornier Metallbauten GmbH. In order to circumvent the constraints forced on the Germans by the Treaty of Versailles, Dornier resolved to open branches of his company in other countries. In Italy he established CMASA (*Societa di Costruzioni Meccaniche Aeronautiche S.A.*) in Marina di Pisa, which was to manufacture flying boats based on the Gs II design. On 6th November 1922 the prototype of the Dornier Wal (Whale) flying boat was first flown. It was to bring Dornier international fame, and was produced under licence in Japan, the Netherlands and Spain. Besides his branch in Italy, Dornier also founded similar plants in Spain, Switzerland and Japan. The Swiss-based facility, which was located in Altenrhein, across Lake Constance from his main office in Germany, became Dornier's premier construction plant for flying boats. There, the Dornier X was built, then the largest flying boat in the world, powered by 12 engines (mounted in six separate tandem nacelles on top of the wing). The first prototype of this giant design (of 56,000 kg take-off weight) lifted off from the surface of Lake Constance for its maiden flight on 12th July 1929. In the ensuing years two more machines of this type, based on orders from Italy, were built.

More experimental designs by Dornier followed. Among them was a twin-engined night bomber, ordered by Japan and designated Do N, which was later produced in cooperation with the Kawasaki company. On 31st March 1930 the first of two prototypes of the Do P four-engined heavy bomber was test-flown. Then, on 17th October 1931, a prototype of the Do Y three-engined bomber took to the air for the first time.

In 1931 Dornier set about designing the Do F twin-engined bomber. It was first flown

on 7th May 1932 in Altenrhein. Its fuselage was of all-metal, stressed-skin construction. The wings were fitted with metal spars and ribs, and covered partially with fabric. The aircraft was powered by two 600 hp Bristol Jupiter radial engines, produced under licence by Siemens. The Do 11 (which was the official designation for the Do F) was included in the 1932-1938 expansion plan for the German Air Force. The production of the Do 11 and Militär-Wal 33 flying boat was undertaken by the Dornier company (which around that time was re-named Dornier-Werke GmbH) in 1933.

When, in January 1933, the National Socialists seized power, the German Air Force entered a period of rapid expansion. On 5th May 1933 the State Ministry of Aviation (*Reichsluftfahrtministerium* or RLM) was formed, with Hermann Göring at its head, and Erhard Milch as the State Secretary for Aviation. The RLM quickly devised a new expansion programme, which aimed at creating a fleet of 400 bombers – the Luftwaffe's main striking force – by the end of 1935.

A technical specification for a *Kampfzerstörer*, a fast assault/bomber aircraft, was created in Obstlt. Wilhelm Wimmer's *Waffenprüfwesen* (weapon test division), which was part of the *Heereswaffenamt* (Ordnance Department) of the *Reichswehrministerium* (Reich Defence Ministry), as early as July 1932. At that time Germany was still under close scrutiny from the international community. Hence, Gen. Lt. von Vollard-Bockelburg, then at the head of the *Heereswaffenamt*, concealed the aircraft's intended role by issuing specifications for a *Schnellverkehrsflugzeug für die DLH* (fast communication aircraft for the DLH)[3]. However, there was no doubt that the design was to be a combat aircraft. Its civilian use was

Interior of Do 17 E-1's rear fuselage. Hydraulic shock-absorber and tailwheel retraction gear.

BMW VI 7,3 engine being coupled to Do 17 E-1's airframe.

BMW VI 7,3 engine, which powered the Do 17 E-1.

responsibilities of the *Reichskommissariat für die Luftfahrt*. Immediate control over the development of new aircraft designs was placed with the *Abteilung Technik* (technical division) of the *Allgemeines Luftamt*, the civilian department of the RLM, under Obstlt. Wilhelm Wimmer.

On 23rd March 1933 Erhard Milch, the *Staatssekretär der Luftfahrt* of the RLM, placed an order with Dornier for two aircraft designated Do 17, one in military configuration, and the other for Lufthansa. It was stressed that the civilian version was to be easily modified for military use. The first prototype of the military version was designated Do 17 C, W.Nr. 256 (later Do 17 V1). The prototype of the civilian version was initially designated Do 17 A, W.Nr. 257 (later Do 17 V2). Both aircraft were to be powered by BMW VI (Do 17 C) or BMW VI 6.0 (Do 17 A) inline engines. On 2nd October 1933 Dornier proposed a third prototype powered by Hispano-Suiza 12Ybrs engines, which was to serve as a 'fast airliner'. On 4th November 1933 the RLM signed the contract, and the aircraft received the designation Do 17 D.

The Do 17 was a markedly advanced design for the first half of the thirties. The airframe was composed of four main sub-parts: the fuselage front and rear sections, the wings and empennage. Its fuselage was a metal monocoque of built-up frames and intermediate stiffeners notched to receive channel-section stringers, and its wing was a two-spar trapezoidal structure, the spar booms being thick duralumin extrusions of asymmetrical section, the girder-type spar bracing utilising duralumin members of broad channel section, from which the main ribs were built up, and the intermediate ribs had a tubular bracing. Wing skinning was flush-riveted light metal, apart from the undersurface of the wing between the spars, for which fabric covering was employed.

The Do 17 C prototype was designed to feature the classic, single tailfin configuration, whilst the Do 17 A prototype was to be equipped with twin tailfins, successfully used by Dornier on his Do 23 bomber. All fuel was housed in the wing centre section, between the engine nacelles and the fuselage, and the main undercarriage members retracted aft hydraulically and mechanically into the tails of the engine nacelles.

The most remarkable characteristic of the new aircraft was the inordinately slim contouring of the fuselage; a pencil-like impression enhanced by a long ogival nose, with, as initially flown, no protuberance other than a shallow flight deck windscreen to mar the lines. This slimness was, in fact, somewhat illusory, as, in planform, the near-cylindrical cross section translated to what can only be described as an inverted triangle, about twice as wide at the top as at the bottom, the sloping sides of which resulted in an abnormally "broad" centre section.

of minor importance, and allowed only if the aircraft could be quickly and inexpensively reconverted to its military version. Invitations to tender were sent to three companies: Dornier, Junkers and Heinkel. The design bureaus eagerly accepted the challenge to create an aircraft that would meet the demands stated by the Army. Thus, three bombers were designed: the Dornier Do 17, the Junkers Ju 86 and the Heinkel He 111.

Of the three producers, Dornier seemed the least concerned about the aircraft's secondary use as a civilian machine. His design, which incorporated all the latest achievements in aerodynamics, featured an unusually slim, long and narrow fuselage, which could accommodate two bomb bays, but had hardly enough room for its six passengers. In March 1933 Dornier prepared a full-scale wooden mock-up. On 17th March 1933 it was demonstrated to representatives of the *Reichskommissariat für die Luftfahrt* (Reich Commissariat for Aviation). On 5th May 1933 the newly established RLM took over the

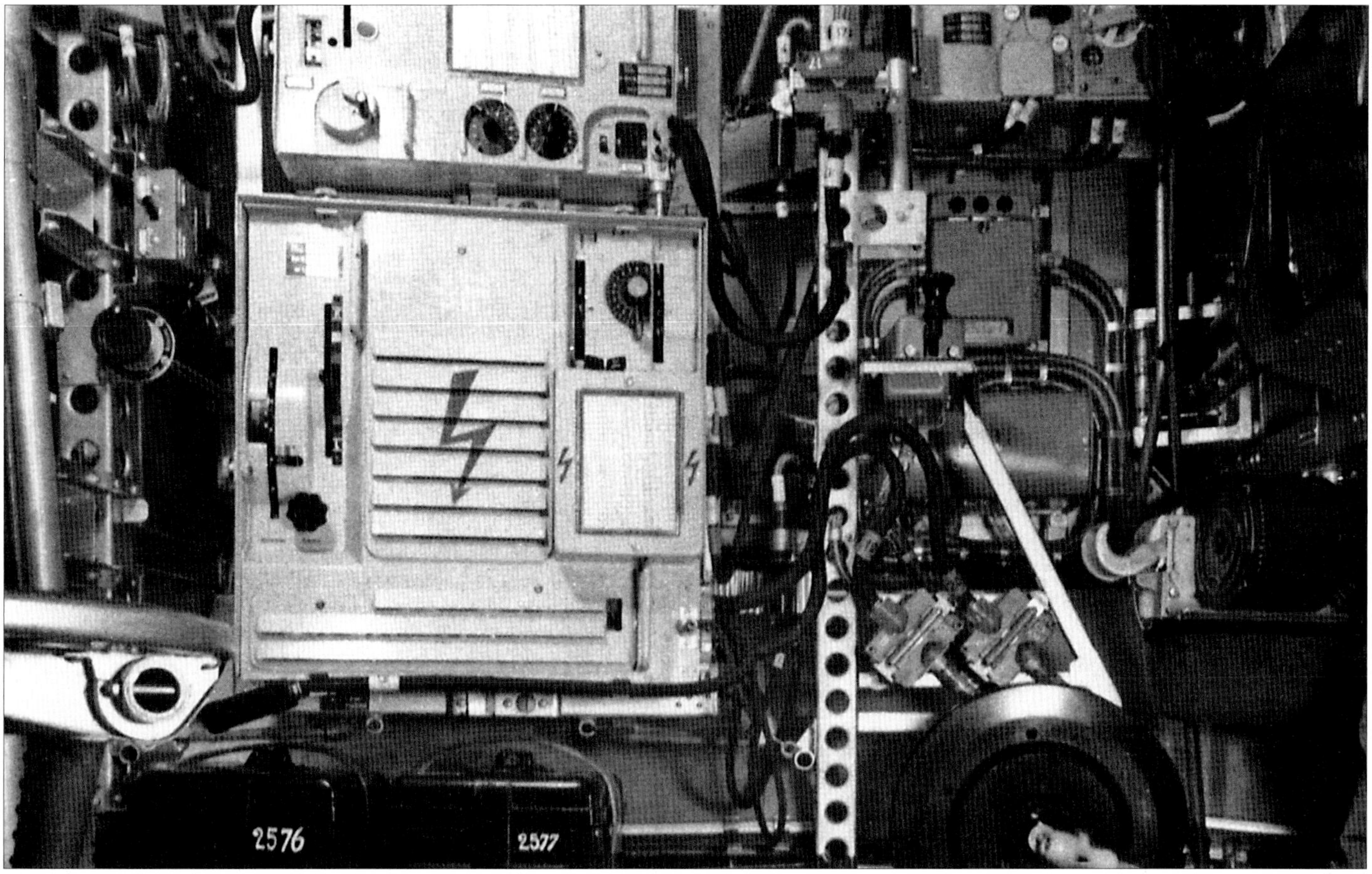

Radio operator's station in Do 17 E-1.

Do 17 E-1's rear upper gun station was armed with 7,92 mm MG 15 machine gun.

Dornier Do 17 E-1 (D-ADNS) at a factory airfield after a test flight.

Experimental Dornier Do 17 E (D-AYZE) powered by BMW Bramo 323 radials.

Aft of the wing, the fuselage transformed once more from elliptical to circular cross section.

The Do 17 C had provision for two bomb magazines, which, arranged in tandem asymmetrically to starboard, could each accommodate five 50 kg bombs hung vertically. The crew comprised three members consisting of a pilot seated asymmetrically to port, with a navigator/bomb aimer seated immediately aft, and a radio operator/gunner accommodated behind the wing trailing edge. This last-mentioned crew member was intended to operate a dorsal machine gun on an open ring mount between frames 17 and 19, as well as a ventral gun firing through a hatch between frames 19 and 21. This defensive armament was, incidentally, specified in a memorandum, which, following discussions held on 20 May 1933, referred to the guns by the cover-name of *Spritzen* (syringes)! Four portholes were inserted in each side of the fuselage aft of the wing trailing edge to afford the radio operator/gunner some measure of vision.[4]

Prototypes and Serial Production Variants

Dornier Do 17 V1

On 20th November 1934 the Do 17 C prototype passed the acceptance tests. It was powered by two BMW VI 7.3 engines, each rated at 500 hp (at 1,390 rpm), with maximum power output of 700 hp (at 1,550 rpm). The engines were fitted with three-blade, two-pitch propellers. The aircraft was unarmed. It featured a conventional, single tailfin and four glazed apertures on either side of the fuselage mid-section to offer the radio operator some field of vision.

Three days later, on 23rd November 1934, Dornier's chief test-pilot Flugkapitän Egon Fath, took the aircraft up for its maiden flight. It was satisfactorily concluded, and by the end of February 1935 the Do 17 C was dispatched to the *Erprobungsstelle Rechlin* (Test Station at Rechlin, usually referred to as *E-Stelle Rechlin*). In mid-February 1935, during one of the evaluation flights, the undercarriage failed on landing and

the machine was damaged. It was repaired by 18th March 1935 and submitted to a series of tests at Rechlin. By then the aircraft was officially designated Do 17 V1.

In late April 1935 another landing gear failure brought the aircraft down for a belly landing. Between 24th and 26th June 1935 the Do 17 V1 was test-flown, along with the Do 17 V2, the other prototype, at Friedrichshafen by two pilots from Rechlin, *Flugkapitäne* Fleischhauer and Thönes. As a result of those tests, the control surface areas were enlarged, and the landing gear wheel struts were set at a different angle for improved stability on landing.

The results of the tests, carried out up to that point, were discussed during a meeting held on 19th July 1935, and the following refinements were postulated:

"1. The radio operator and rear gun stations ought to be moved two segments forward, from the section between the 15th and 17th formers to the section between the 13th and 15th formers.

2. The rear bomb bay ought to be moved forward, from the section between the 13th and 15th formers to the section between the 9th and 11th formers.[5]"

A transparent fairing, which afforded the radio operator a field of vision and fire for his machine gun, replaced the eight glazed apertures, which, after relocation of the radio operator's station, were no longer of any use.

On 30th October 1935 the Do 17 V1, civil registration D-AJUN, returned to Rechlin, where further service evaluations were conducted. On 21st December 1935, during a low-level flight, one of the aircraft's engines stalled. The V1 clipped the ground with its wingtip and

crashed. Of the four-man crew, two were seriously injured. The aircraft was written off. Tests were continued with W.Nr. 686 "Ersatz V1" (V1 replacement), which received the same registration code D-AJUN. It was first flown on 13th June 1936. The aircraft was powered by BMW VI 7.3 engines and fitted with twin tailfins. It was later used as a test-bed for Elvemag (*Elektr. Vertikalmagazine*) bomb racks, mounted vertically inside the fuselage.

Dornier Do 17 V2

Unlike the Do 17 C, the Dornier Do 17 A, W.Nr. 257 was to prototype a civilian version. Designated Do 17 V2, it first flew on 5th May 1935. Viewed as essentially a 'demilitarised' model, the Do 17 V2 actually differed from the V1 in a number of respects. It was powered by two BMW VI 6.3 engines, each rated at 640 hp at 1,530 rpm, and driving two– or three-bladed, two-pitch propellers. The capacity of each of the two centre section fuel tanks was increased from 500 to 700 litres. Apart from the provision of commercial radio equipment, the flight deck had been extensively revised in conformity with Lufthansa requests, full dual control being introduced and the cabin roof being raised to provide additional headroom and improve forward vision. Other changes included the introduction of cut-outs in the main-wheel well doors, through which the wheels protruded when retracted, and the insertion of rectangular windows in the sloping sides of the fuselage beneath and immediately forward of the wing, the aft portholes being deleted.[6]

Dornier's factory documentation includes information, rarely mentioned by most authors,

Dornier Do 17 E-1 of 7./KG 255 during 1938 summer manoeuvres. Of note are temporary markings in form of red discs, which replaced regular crosses. An excellent view of the three-colour splinter camouflage used by the Luftwaffe in late 30-ties of the 20th century.

MONOGRAFIE MONOGRAPHS

that the Do 17 V2 was fitted with three passenger compartments. Hence, it could carry a total of ten, besides its two-man crew. A room was made for two passengers between the pilots' cockpit and the front spar. Four more could be seated between the front and main spars, albeit in a compartment only 140 cm high! It could be entered via a ladder and a hatch located in the lower part of the fuselage. Four more passenger seats were planned behind the main spar. The machine was test-flown at the factory airfield, whereupon it received the civilian registration D-AHAK "Rhein" and was transferred to Lufthansa for further evaluation. The ensuing tests took only a month, from 8th October to 7th November 1935. Lufthansa rejected the aircraft as unsuitable for its designed role of a fast courier machine. The passenger compartment, with wing spars running across it, was deemed to be too uncomfortable. Another major inconvenience was the fact that the main luggage compartment could only be accessed from the top of the fuselage. The aircraft was returned to Friedrichshafen, where it was turned into a prototype of the Do 17 E bomber.

Re-engined with the BMW VI 7.3 units, the rebuilt Do 17 V2 featured the definitive forward fuselage and crew arrangement. Flown in its new guise for the first time on 7th May 1936, and delivered to Rechlin two weeks later, on 20th May, the Do 17 V2 may be considered to have initiated the German predilection for grouping all crewmembers in the forward fuselage. The radio compartment, now moved forward to a position immediately aft of the navigator's station, was surmounted by a blister fairing containing the flexible mounting for an aft-firing 7.92 mm MG 15 machine gun and a similar weapon could be fired through a hatch in the floor.[7]

Dornier Do 17 V3

On 28th February 1935 it was decided to couple the Do 17 D, now carrying the designation Do 17 V3, to BMW VI 7.3 engines, instead of the planned Hispano-Suiza HS 12Ybrs, which were not available. The first flight of the Dornier Do 17 V3, W.Nr. 258, D-ABIH, took place on 19th September 1935, with *Flugkapitän* Egon Fath at the controls. The aircraft was fitted with a KLs/A17 flexible mount for a 20 mm Borsig LB 204 cannon. In November 1935 a machine so armed flew to Rechlin, and later was transferred to an ordnance test station at Travemünde.

Dornier Do 17 V4 to V14

The fourth prototype was the Do 17 V4, W.Nr. 654, D-AGYA, first flown on 24th March 1936. Initially planned as a civilian machine, it was eventually fitted with a 20 mm Borsig LB 204

cannon on KLs/A17 mount and used as a weapons test-bed. A two-cannon configuration was also considered, but apparently it never advanced beyond the study stage. In the period between June 1936 and June 1937 the aircraft was tested at Tarnewitz and Travemünde.

The Do 17 V5, W.Nr. 655, D-AKOH, was to prototype serial-production communication aircraft for Lufthansa. It was powered by boosted Hispano-Suiza 12Ykrs engines, rated at 775 hp on take-off, and with maximum output of 860 hp at 4,000 metres, which allowed the aircraft to reach a speed of 391 kph. Notably, at that time the top speed of the British Gloster Gauntlet fighter, which equipped the Royal Air Force, was barely 370 kph. Despite the aircraft's impressive performance, Lufthansa was not interested in it for the above-mentioned reasons.

BMW VI 7.3 engines rated at 750 hp on take-off powered the Do 17 V6, W.Nr. 656, D-AKUZ. It could carry up to six passengers. It was first flown on 12th October 1936. Later it was pressed into service with the Luftwaffe as a fast transport (*Reiseflugzeug*) coded GL+AJ. It is known to have remained with II./LG 1 stationed at Beaumont until 3rd April 1943.

The Do 17 V7, W.Nr. 657, D-AQYK, prototyped the E-2 bomber version with a new, rounded and extensively glazed, 'greenhouse' nose. It completed its maiden flight on 10th December 1936. Meanwhile, the Dornier Do 17 V8, W.Nr. 658, D-AXON, took to the air for the first time on 10th September 1936. It was a prototype of a long-range reconnaissance version, designated the F-1. Shortly afterwards it was re-engined with Daimler-Benz DB 600 inline engines rated at 1,000 hp on take-off. The recon-

Do 17M advertising photo.

Dornier Do 17 E-1 of JFS 4 at Fürth airbase, 1941.

Pilot's and gunner's stations in Dornier Do 17 E-1. Note two 7.92 mm MG 15 machine guns on flexible mounts.

structed airframe received a new serial number (W.Nr. 691) and registration (D-AELE).

Between 22nd July and 1st August 1937 the aircraft participated in the IV Internationales Flugmeeting at Dübendorf airbase, near Zurich, Switzerland. On that occasion it was designated Do 17 MV1 and fitted with the then latest, pre-production Daimler-Benz DB 601 A-0 inline engines (of 33,390 cmł displacement and 1,100 hp output on take-off). There were 60 participant aircraft from 14 countries. The Do 17 MV1, flown by *Flugkapitän* Polte, caused quite a sensation. During the speed race it achieved an impressive 425 kph. The Do 17

MV1 also won the first place in the *Alpenrundflug* Category B – a round, 367-kilometre trip over the Alps. The winning aircraft was crewed by none other than *General der Flieger* Erhard Milch (commander), Major Polte (pilot), Fl-Ing. Hänsgen (radio operator) oraz Fl-Ing. Franz (flight engineer).

After the return to Germany the aircraft was again rebuilt. Fitted with a round, glazed bomber nose and coded GL+AL, at the turn of 1939/40 it served as a test-bed in Rechlin. In October 1940, equipped with a K4ü autopilot, it was stationed at Staaken. In early 1941, under the civilian registration D-AELE, it was

A hangar used by one of German flight schools, with Dornier Do 17 E-1 visible in the background.

Dornier Do 17 E-1 'Habicht' (Pike) of II./KG 255, Germany 1938.

relocated to Ainring and used for trials towing DSF gliders.

The Dornier Do 17 V9, W.Nr. 659, D-ABOY, was finished in V6 configuration. In factory documentation it was referred to as a *Sonderflugzeug* (special purpose aircraft) and was used by the Dornier company for testing various equipment and as a courier aircraft.

The Do 17 V10, W.Nr. 660, D-AKUU, later RB+DK (first flown on 21st October 1936) and V11, W.Nr. 681, D-ATYA (first flown on 11th February 1936) were both prototypes of the F-1 long-range reconnaissance version.

The Do 17 V12, W.Nr. 682, D-AKYU, was to be another prototype of the E-2 version, but eventually it was used to test the new Daimler-

Dornier Do 17 E-1s of 3./KG 255 (note the unit's emblem under cockpit). In the background the aircraft coded 54+K13.

Benz DB 600 C engines rated at 1,050 hp on take-off, and first flown in October 1936. Initially the DB 600 engines were also to power the Do 17 V13, W.Nr. 683, D-ATAH, but ultimately Bramo 323 A-1 engines were mounted instead. The Do 17 V14, W.Nr. 684, D-AFOU, took to the air for the first time on 7th April 1937. It was powered by Bramo 323 D engines. Equipped with photographic cameras, it later served with *Lichtbildsonderstaffel Rowehl*, a secret photo-re-connaissance squadron commanded by Obst. Theodor Rowehl.

Long-range reconnaissance Dornier Do 17 F-1 in pre-war painting scheme on an airfield in central Germany.

Dornier Do 17 E/F

Serial production of Do 17 E bombers and Do 17 F reconnaissance aircraft commenced in late 1936 at Dornier plants in Manzell, Allmansweiller and Löwenthal. The first pre-production model was the Do 17 E-0 powered by BMW VI 7.3 engines producing 750 horsepower on take-off, which drove VDM three-blade propellers of 3.20 m in diameter. Total capacity of the wing-mounted fuel tanks was 1,400 litres. The crew comprised pilot, navigator and radio operator/rear gunner.

Defensive armament was limited to a single 7.92 mm MG 15 machine gun on a flexible mount, located in the B-Stand on the fuselage spine, directly aft of the cabin. Offensive armament was 500 kg of bombs (or 750 kg with less fuel onboard), carried in two fuselage bomb bays on RAW 14 (*Reihenabwurfgerät*) racks. The payload was usually ten SC 50, four SC 100, or two SC 250 bombs. Lotfe C7A or Goerz GVZ 19d bomb sights were used.

The serial-production Do 17 E-1 was identical to the E-0. Later on, some aircraft were upgunned with a 7.92 mm MG 15 machine gun in the nose, and another MG 15, on a flexible mount, in the crew compartment's floor. The E-1 airframe was also utilized to manufacture the Do-17 F-1 long-range reconnaissance version. The F-1 was equipped with Rb 10/18, Rb 20/30 and Rb 50/30 photographic cameras apiece, mounted in place of bomb bays. The navigator handled another hand-operated camera. Radio equipment included FuG IIIaU, Peil GV and FuBl 1 sets. The aircraft could also carry Blitzlichtbomben LC 50 F flares for night photography.

Exact production numbers of the Do 17 E/F versions remain unclear. Dornier's own plant assembled 328 aircraft of the E model and a further 77 of the F, for a total of 405 machines. However, several dozen more were probably manufactured by the Henschel plant in Berlin-

Dornier Do 17 V2 BMW VI 6,3 engines rated at 640 hp, driving two-blade propellers.

Dornier Do 17 Ka from Yugoslav order.

Schönefeld and by Siebel in Halle. Some sources claim that the total number of the two models was 536.

Whilst serial production of the Do 17 E/F was in progress, some aircraft were rebuilt as test-beds. The Dornier Do 17 V15, W.Nr. 816, was equipped with a five-man crew compartment as well as additional radio and navigation equipment. It served as *Führungsflugzeug* (command aircraft) with a Lehrgeschwader (training wing) stationed at Greifswald. The Do 17 V16, W.Nr. 839, was earmarked for testing DB 600 and 601 engines, but eventually it was equipped with BMW VI 7.3 powerplants and used for experimenting with an electrical system of fusing bombs. The Do 17 V17, W.Nr. 801, in turn, served as a test platform for radio equipment and de-icer systems.

The E-1 was expected to be succeeded by the E-2. However, the latter was not serial-produced. The three known aircraft to have received the E-2 designation were D-AADO, D-AIDO and D-AOFU. They were passed to the DVL and Hansa-Luftbild GmbH. The Do 17 E-3 also did not make it to series production. The only E-3, registered as D-AOTI, was run by the DVL. The photo-reconnaissance Do 17 F-2 did not enter production either. The only F-2, registered as D-ACZJ, served as a test aircraft for the Carl Zeiss-Jena optical works.

In October 1937 the E model airframe was used to build two prototypes – the Do 17 V18, W.Nr. 2021 and V19, W.Nr. 2022 – powered by nine-cylinder, air-cooled, radial BMW 132 F engines, which were developed from American-made Pratt & Whitney 'Hornets'. The two ma-

Do 17 Ka was powered by Mistral Major radials.

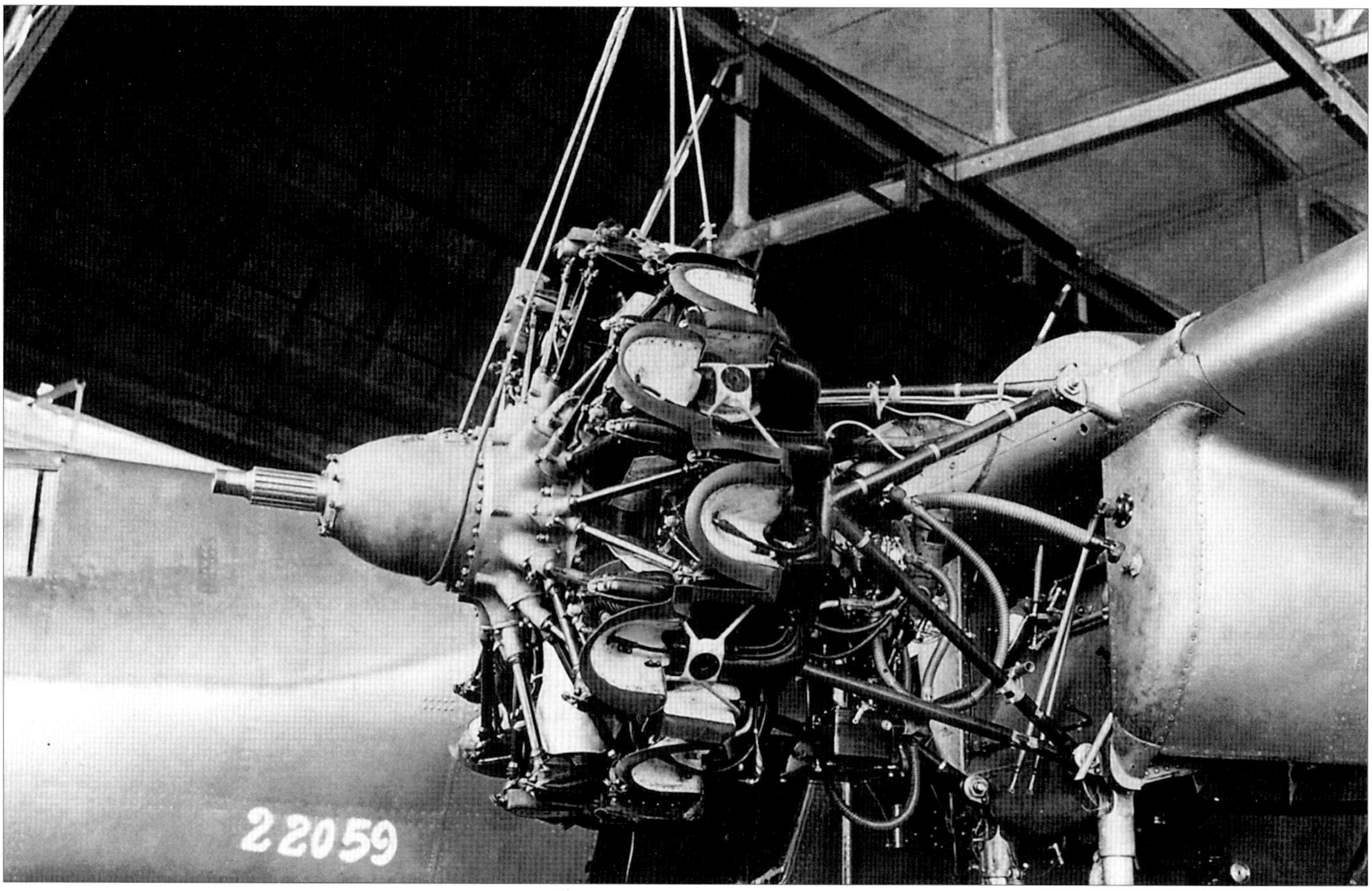

22059

chines were later designated Do 17 J-1 and J-2, respectively. Other experimental aircraft based on the E model airframe were the Do 17 V20, W.Nr. 2031 and V21, W.Nr. 2032, powered by nine-cylinder, radial Bramo 323 F Fafnir engines. These two aircraft were subsequently designated Do 17 L-1 and L-2, respectively.

Dornier Do 17 Ka and Kb

The success of the Do 17 MV1 at the Flugmeeting in Dübendorf resulted in a contract being signed with Yugoslavia for the delivery of 36 Do 17 K aircraft for the JKRV (Royal Yugoslav Air Force). This export version was based on the E-1 airframe. It featured the distinctive, pointed nose of Do 17 MV1. It was powered by 14-cylinder, two-row, air-cooled radial French Gnôme-Rhône 14K engines rated at 870 hp on take-off, driving three-blade, metal VDM propellers of 3.30 m in diameter.

Yugoslavia ordered 20 Do 17Ka-1 bombers equipped with Viro bombing sights and Trahan bomb racks. Fourteen aircraft were Do 17 Ka-2 reconnaissance machines fitted with Lešner or Nistri cameras. The aircraft destined for Yugoslavia received FuG III Telefunken 274af and P 63uN radio sets. Their armament consisted of three Belgian 7.7 mm FN-Browning machine guns on flexible mounts, of which two fired rearward (in dorsal and ventral positions) and one forward, on the starboard side of the windscreen. The first machine from the JKRV contract made its maiden flight in Manzell on 6th October 1937. Three weeks later, on 25th October 1935, *Flugkapitän* Egon Fath delivered it to Belgrade. The two remaining machines (of the order of 36), designated Do 17 Kb-1, were based on the then latest M (bomber) version. They served as production prototypes for a planned production run of 100 machines, manufactured

under licence in the Yugoslav State Aircraft Factory (Državna Fabrika Aviona) at Kraljevo. The licence aircraft were powered by Gnôme-Rhône 14 Na engines rated at 980 hp on take-off, produced by a local factory at Rakovica near Belgrade. The commencement of the Do 17 Kb-1's serial production in Krajlevo was delayed, and the first licence-built aircraft was not ready until early 1940. Eventually, only 40 were manufactured in Yugoslavia before the German invasion, which started on 6th April 1941.

Dornier Do 17 M/P

The Do 17 M/P were development versions of the Do 17 E/F. Despite what its designation might suggest, the race-winning Do 17 MV1, W.Nr. 691, was not the prototype of the M model. The Do 17 M was in fact prototyped by two

Dornier Do 17 Kb-1 manufactured on licence in Yugoslavia.

Do 17M, Paris 25 November – 11 December 1939.

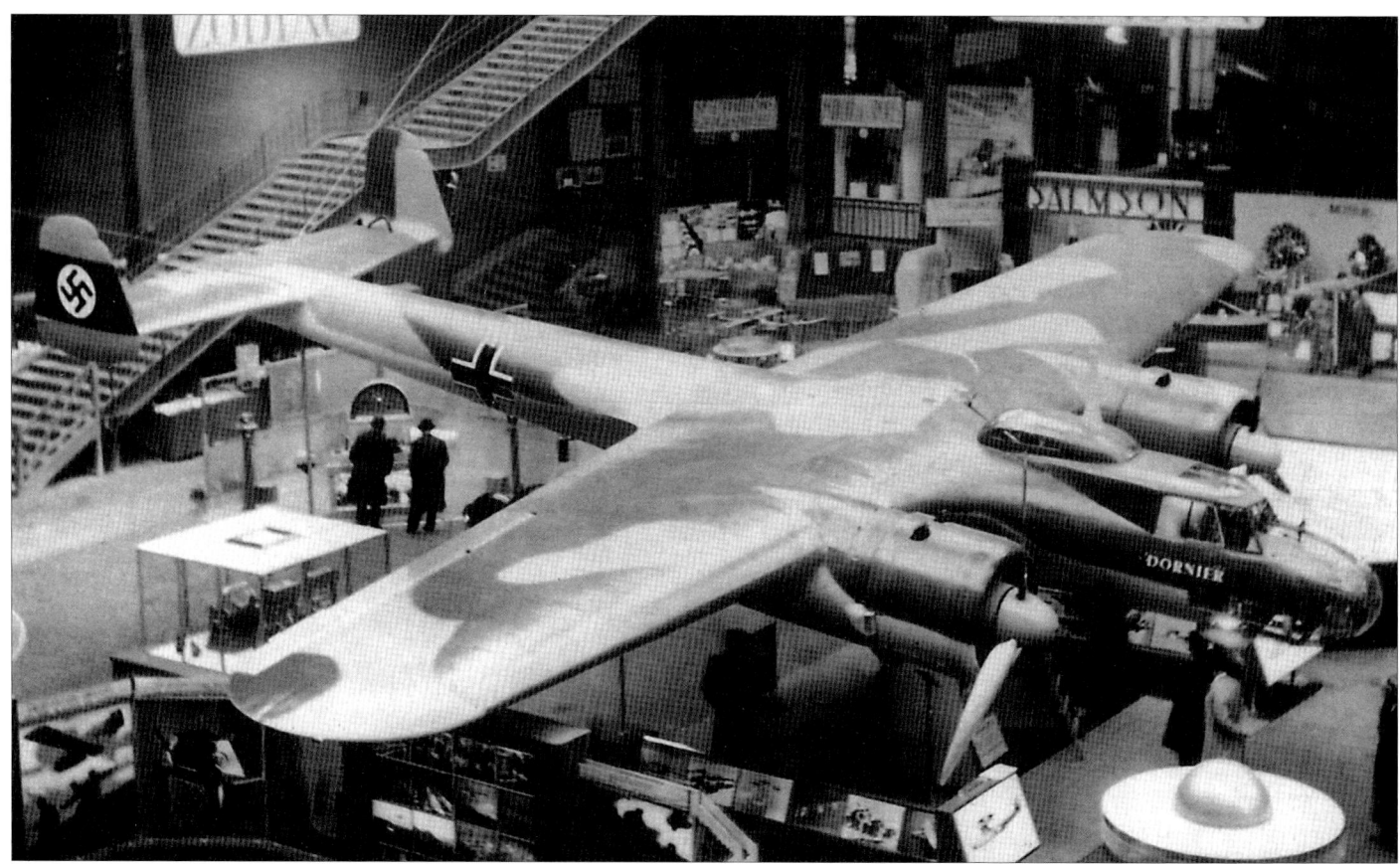

Dornier Do 17 M presented to the public at Paris Air Salon, which was held from 25th November to 11th December 1938.

aircraft: the Do 17 MV2, W.Nr. 692, D-AUQO, powered by Bramo 323 A radials, and the Do 17 MV3, W.Nr. 693, D-AAQU, coupled to Bramo 323 D engines.

The airframe remained basically that of the E-1, the major difference being the new power-plants, the Bramo 323 A-1 rated at 900 hp on take-off, which drove three-blade, metal VDM propellers of 3.60 m in diameter. Unlike the E/F models, the wing-mounted fuel cells (of 1,910-litre capacity) in the Do 17 M were self-sealing. It was also equipped with a de-icer installation, based on an exhaust heat exchanger in the wing leading edges. In order to dampen vibration,

Cockpit details of the Do 17 M presented at Paris.

the engines were mounted on metal-rubber bearers. The wings featured all-metal skinning (in the E/F models they were partially covered with fabric). Radio equipment included FuG II-IaU, Peil GV, E.V., and Fu.Bl. 1 sets. The Siemens-produced autopilot was also at hand. Offensive armament consisted of a 1,000 kg bombload. Defensive armament comprised three 7.92 mm MG 15 machine guns on flexible mounts. The Dornier-München plant built a total of 200 aircraft of this version.

The Do 17 M-1 airframe was used to create the long-range reconnaissance Do-17 P-1. The latter was designed around BMW 132 N-1 engines, which delivered 910 hp on take-off, and drove three-blade, metal VDM propellers of 3.70 m in diameter. Fuel capacity was increased to 2,095 litres. Fuel was stored in self-sealing tanks, two in the wings (2 x 760 litres) and two more in the fuselage (1 x 350 litres and 1 x 225 litres). Instead of bomb bays, the aircraft's fuselage housed one Rb 10/18, one Rb 20/30 and one Rb 50/30 photographic camera. As in the Do 17 F-1, the observer was also equipped with a hand-held camera. The Do 17 P-2 sub-variant could alternatively, in place of the Rb 50/30 camera, carry four 20 kg parachute flares. During the war some aircraft underwent field modifications. The Do 17 M-1/U1 was fitted with an inflatable life raft stored inside the fuselage. Aircraft operating in Africa were equipped with anti-dust filters and emergency landing survival kits (a rifle, water and food). Such modified machines were designated Do 17 M-1/trop and Do 17 P-1/trop. A total of 330 Do 17 Ps were produced, this number including eight by Dornier, 100 by Henschel, 149 by the HFB plant, and 73 by Siebel.

Dornier Do 17 R

Four M model airframes (W.Nr. 2194 through 2197), registered as D-AORT, D-ARZI, D-ATJU and D-AWIS, were rebuilt as fast, long-range reconnaissance aircraft (Do 17 R1-R4), for employment with *Lichtbildsonderstaffel Rowehl*. They were powered by DB 601 B engines rated at 1,100 hp (which was nearly 200 hp more than the output of the Bramo 323 A-1 powerplants), which allowed them to attain a top speed of 532 kph (as compared to 410 kph for the Do 17 P-1). The engines drove three-blade, metal VDM propellers of 3.40 m in diameter. The aircraft's range remained unchanged, but its operational ceiling increased from 6,400 to 9,000 metres. The fuselage housed three photographic cameras (2 x Rb 20/30 and 1 x Rb 50/30). The aircraft

Do 17F of III/KG 255, during exercise in 1938.

were stripped of all defensive armament to save weight.

Dornier Do 17 S

Another modification specifically designed for *Lichtbildsonderstaffel Rowehl* was the Do 17 S, built in only three pieces (S-1 through S-3). These aircraft featured a completely redesigned, pod-like cockpit, known as a *Waffenkopf*, which offered the crew more room and better visibility. The roof was extended upward over the line of the fuselage, sloping down to meet it just in front of the wing. The dorsal gun was moved to the rear of the pod where it had a considerably better field of fire. Likewise, the floor was dropped under the fuselage and the ventral gun moved to the back of the pod, allowing it to fire directly to the rear. The Do 17 S was powered by DB 601 A inline engines.[8] Like its predecessor the Do 17 R, the S model was unarmed.

Dornier Do 17 U

Some aircraft of the S model (15 in all) were rebuilt as command aircraft (*Führungsflugzeug*) and designated Do 17 U. Three Do 17 U-0 pre-production machines were powered by DB 601

A inline engines, whilst the remaining 12 (designated Do 17 U-1) were given Bramo 323 A-1 radials. The enlarged *Waffenkopf* front section housed a crew of six (a second radio operator included) and was equipped with a hinged chart table. Radio equipment comprised FuG X, Peil GV and Fu.Bl. 1 sets. The four fuel tanks (two in the wings, and two in the fuselage) had a total capacity of 2,260 litres. Since much of the fuselage space was occupied by fuel cells, the U model could not carry bombs. Standard defensive armament consisted of three 7.92 mm MG 15 machine guns on flexible mounts, with provision for two additional MG 15 guns firing out of the sides of the upper part of the pod (however, as the three guns were all manned by a single gunner, only one of them could be fired at a time).

Dornier Do 17 Z

Since DB 601 inline engines were slated for fighter aircraft, the next development version of the Do 17 was equipped with Bramo 323 A-1 radials, which drove three-blade VDM propellers. The prototype, designated Do 17 ZV1, W.Nr. 2180, D-ABVD, first flew on 1st March 1938. It was the production prototype for both the Do 17 Z-0 (a short pre-production run), and the Do 17 Z-1 (the first large-scale production sub-variant). The new version was based on the M model airframe with an enlarged *Waffenkopf* nose section, which could house a crew of four. Due to the aircraft's re-designed front section, its engines and main landing gear wheels were set wider apart. Defensive armament in the Z-0 remained unchanged (as compared to the M model) and comprised three 7.92 mm MG 15 machine guns on flexible mounts, whilst the Z-1 sub-variant was upgunned with an additional MG 15 mounted in the front section (for the bombardier). However, the increase in weight meant the bombload was reduced to 500 kg. Bombsights were Lotfe A or B types. With time all Do 17 Z-1 aircraft in frontline service were upgraded to the Z-2 standard.

The inferior performance of the Z-1 was addressed in the next major production model, the Do 17 Z-2, which was powered by Bramo 323 P-1 engines equipped with two-stage superchargers and rated at 1,000 hp. This allowed the bombload to be increased back to 1,000 kg (usually 20 x SC 50 or 4 x SC 250 bombs), albeit at the cost of the aircraft's combat range, which, with the maximum bombload was a very short 205 miles (330 km). Bomb racks were of Träg 5 Schloß 50/IX and EHVC 500/VIII types. If the bombload was reduced by half, the aircraft could carry an additional 895-litre fuel tank rigged in the front bomb bay, which increased the aircraft's range to 1,150 km. Defensive armament consisted of

Mechanics at the engine of a Dornier Do 17P.

Airbrakes intended for the Do 217 during tests on a Do 17M.

Dornier Do 17M after a force landing.

six 7.92 mm MG 15 machine guns. Despite the increase in its take-off weight to over 8,800 kg, the Do 17 Z-2 attained a top speed of 421 kph, which made it the fastest bomber version of the Do 17 built thus far.

Modifications to the basic Z-2 model included the Z-3 sub-variant called a *Stabsstaffeler-kunder* (HQ flight's scout), which was a bomber-reconnaissance version. These aircraft were tasked with documenting the results of bombing raids. The Z-3's powerplants, defensive armament and basic equipment were identical to the Z-2, with the exception of added survival kit for over-water flights. Two photographic cameras (Rb 20/30 and Rb 30/50) could be rigged to an entry hatch. In the latter part of 1940 a 15 mm MG 151/15 cannon replaced the front machine gun mounted on the A-Stand gunner station.

Another modification to see service was the Do 17 Z-4 dual-control trainer, usually used for training pilots in 'blind' flying. It did not enter serial production. The severe personnel losses suffered by the Luftwaffe during its operations over the English Channel resulted in the Do 17 Z-5. It was equipped with flotation cells in the fuselage and engine nacelles, in case it was

forced down on water, as well as a radio set with a power generator and a special kite to lift the radio antenna (which gave the radio signals a better range and increased the chances of rescue). A total of 40 Z-5s were produced.

The Do 17 Z-6 was a meteorological reconnaissance variant, created by modifying several Z-1s or Z-2s. The Z-6 was duly fitted with specialist meteorological equipment and additional fuel tanks (at the cost of its bombing capability), which increased its fuel capacity to 2,890 litres. Due to the long high-altitude flights carried out by the Z-6 crews, the number of onboard oxygen bottles was increased from 20 to 24. The water ditching survival kit, which had been introduced with the Z-5, was also included.

Combat experience derived from the Luftwaffe's operations in the first year of the war indicated the need for a ground-attack aircraft, which could carry out low-altitude strikes against the enemy directly on the battlefield or in its immediate rear areas. In response, Dornier designed the *Geier* (Vulture), an assault version of the Do 17 designated Z-8. Nevertheless, it soon transpired that without armour plating to protect the aircraft's most vital mechanisms it was too vulnerable to ground fire. Since the

Dornier Do 17 MV1 fitted with the nose section typical of the K (export) model.

available powerplants were unable to cope with the additional weight of such armour, the project was scrapped.

Instead of producing a specialized assault version, it was decided to modify the Do 17 Z for carrying out low-level, surprise attacks against enemy defensive positions, artillery batteries and troop concentrations. Thus the Do 17 Z-9 came into being. It featured re-designed bomb bays fitted with a total of 16 ELVEMAG 5C10 bomb racks for carrying each five 10 kg SD 10 fragmentation bombs, for a total of 80. The SD 10 bombs were stored vertically and dropped by a RAB 14 c automatic salvo release device. In order to quicken the release of so many bombs, perforated covers replaced the standard bomb bay doors. This sub-variant was not equipped with the water ditching survival kit.

The Z-9 was the last bomber version of the Do 17. Dornier's 'Flying Pencil', as it was nicknamed, was soon phased out in favour of the faster and more capable Junkers Ju 88. During the first months of the war the production of Do 17s considerably decreased, until in summer 1940 it was terminated altogether.

Dornier Do 17 Z-7/-10 night fighters

In the early phase of the Second World War responsibility for night air defence of the Reich was mainly bestowed upon Flak batteries cooperating with searchlights. From September 1939, single-engined fighter aircraft – initially Arado Ar 68 biplanes, later Messerschmitt Bf 109s – were pressed into service as night interceptors. In mid-May 1940 the RAF heavy bombers began to raid the Ruhr Valley at night. The

Dornier Do 17 MV1 fitted with the nose section typical of the K (export) model.

Dornier Do 17 MV1 powered by Daimler-Benz DB 601 A-0 engines proved a real 'star' of the Internationales Flugmeeting held in Switzerland in the summer of 1937.

Daimler-Benz DB 601 A-0 inline engines rated at 1,100 KM enabled the Do 17 MV1 to achieve top speed of 425 kph.

Luftwaffe's high command therefore issued urgent orders to the country's major aircraft producers for the modification of suitable aircraft types to operate as night fighters. Dornier came up with a project designated Do 17 Z-7 "Kauz I" (Screech Owl I).

The Z-7 was converted from existing Z-series airframes and fitted with Bramo 323 P-1 engines rated at 1,000 hp. Its glazed bomber-style nose section was replaced with a solid nose from the Ju 88 C, fitted with a fixed-mount, forward-firing 20 mm MG FF (or 20 mm MG 151/20) cannon and three 7.92 mm MG 17 machine guns. The front gun bay was separated from the crew compartment by an 11 mm armoured bulkhead. Fuel was stored in two wing-mounted tanks (of 770-litre capacity each) and one fuselage tank mounted in the forward bomb bay (of 895-litre capacity). Since it was presumed that night fighter operations would take place at relatively low altitudes, the number of oxygen bottles for the crew of three was reduced from 20 to nine. Defensive armament was limited to two 7.92 mm MG 15 machine guns on flexible mounts (in the B– and C-Stand). An interesting novelty was the *Spanner-Gerät* infrared detection system, which comprised an IF searchlight and a monitor display.

Most probably only three airframes of Z-7 configuration were built. One of them was the machine coded R4+HK of I./NJG 2, which crashed on landing on 9th November 1940.

The Z-7's successor was the Do 17 Z-10 "Kauz II". Only nine aircraft of this sub-variant were converted from existing Z-series airframes. It featured an aerodynamically improved nose section, which provided a housing for an additional fixed 7.92 mm MG 17 machine gun, for a total of one 20 mm cannon (MG FF or MG 151/20) and four 7.92 mm MG 17 machine guns. Standard radio equipment included FuG X, FuG 25, Peil GV i Fu.Bl. 1 sets. The *Spanner-Gerät* infrared device was used only sporadically. In May 1942 at Werneuchen test station one Do 17 Z-10, coded CD+PV, was used as a flying testbed to help develop the FuG 202 "Lichtenstein C-1" airborne radar set.

Do 17 serial production

Serial production of Do 17s commenced at the end of 1936, starting with the E (bomber) and F (reconnaissance) models. At the turn of 1937/38 the Do 17 E was gradually phased out in favour of the M model. Production of the Do 17 P, the reconnaissance version, began in

1938. The most numerous of Do 17 variants was the Z model. Production of Do 17s was carried out in Dornier's own plants as well as by Siebel in Halle, Henschel in Berlin-Schöne- feld, and Hamburger Flugzeugbau in Hamburg. A further 40 Do 17s (of Kb 1 version) were manufactured abroad, in Yugoslavia. The grand total production figure of all Do 17 variants

A production Dornier Do 17 Z-1 with Bramo 323 A-1 engines.

Cockpit of the Dornier Do 17 V2, W.Nr. 257.

Dornier Do 17 M V2, W.Nr. 692 with civil registration D-AUQO.

stood at 2,180 aircraft, this number including the following:
– Do 17 E/F – 536 (including 328 Do 17 Es i 77 Do 17 Fs at Dornier/München)
– Do 17 K – approx. 74 (including 38 in Yugoslavia)
– Do 17 M – 200 (at Dornier/München)
– Do 17 P – 330 (Dornier – 8, Siebel – 73, HFB – 149)
– Do 17 U – 15 (Dornier)
– Do 17 Z – 913 (Dornier – 420, Henschel – 320, HFB – 74, Siebel – 73)

Dornier Do 215

After the Dornier Do 17's outstandingly successful demonstration at the International Flug-meeting in Dübendorf, Yugoslavia was not the only country interested in purchasing the new bomber. Since the Do 17's serial-production models ran from E through Z, the *Reichsluft-fahrtministerium* assigned a new designation – Do 215 – to the export version. It was based on the S model. The first prototype, the Do 215 V1 (civil registration D-AFFY), was lost in 1938 in a crash during one of the test flights.

A pair of Dornier Do 17 E-1 of II./KG 155, based at Ansbach.

French Gnôme-Rhône 14 N radials powered the second prototype, the Do 215 V2, D-AIIB. It was demonstrated to the representatives of the Yugoslavian Air Force. Since it offered no notable performance increase over the Do 17 K already operated by the Yugoslavs, it didn't attract orders. Dornier therefore equipped the Do 215 V3 prototype, coded 25+C03, with 12-cyl-inder Daimler-Benz DB 601 A-1 inline engines rated at 1,100 hp on take-off. Besides more power output, the inline engines produced less drag, which further enhanced the aircraft's performance. The Do 215 V3's maximum speed topped 486 kph, which was 66 kph more than the top speed of the Do 17 Z-2. After presenting the aircraft to several foreign purchasing committees, Sweden decided to buy 18 Do 215s (in place of Breguet Br 694s ordered in France). Series production of the Do 215 A-1, prototyped by the Do 215 V3, for the Swedes began in August 1939. With the outbreak of the Second World War the aircraft were embargoed and pressed into Luftwaffe service. They were designated Do 215 B-0 and B-1.

The Do 215 B-1 was a bomber/long-range reconnaissance aircraft. Its defensive armament comprised four 7.92 mm MG 15 machine guns on

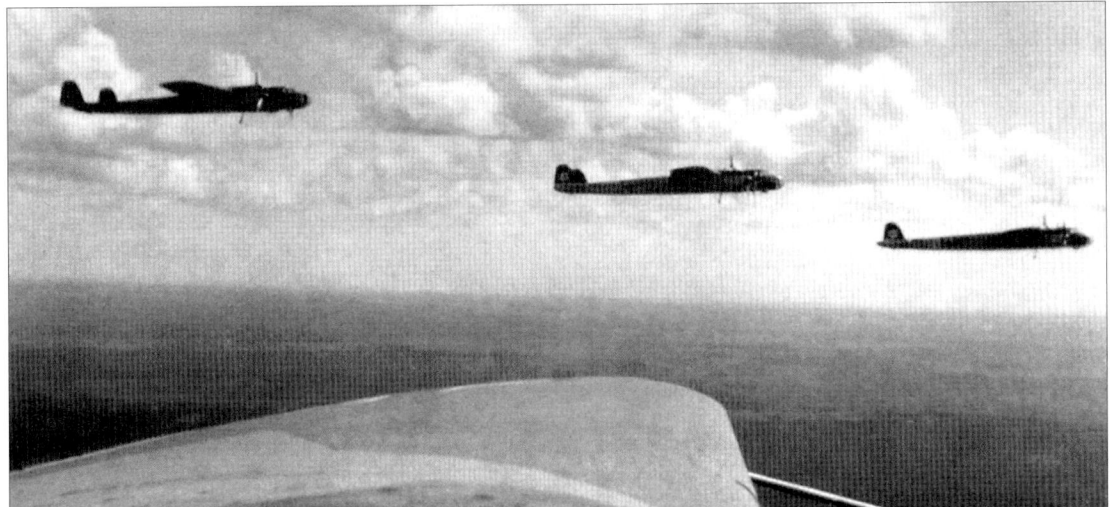

Dornier Do 17 F-1 of 1.(F)/24
at Kassel-Rothwesten airfield.

Dornier Do 17Es
in combat formation.

Details of Bramo 323 A
engine, which powered Do 17
M-1. The engine drove VDM
three-bladed propeller.

One of Do 17 M's prototypes photographed at a factory airfield during engines' check.

flexible mounts. Radio equipment included FuG X, FuG 25, Peil GV i Fu.Bl. 1 sets. The aircraft also carried photographic cameras of various types.

Do 215 B-2, which didn't enter production, was a long-range reconnaissance machine fit-

ted with DB 601 A engines and a sliding cover under the bomb bay, which housed an Rb 50/30 camera. Three more cameras, of Rb 20/30 type, were fixed to the inner side of entry hatch, and another Rb 50/30 camera was located at the B-

Dornier Do 215 B-1, Stammkenzeichen NO + TB during a test flight.

Stand station underneath the fuselage. In view of the successful reconnaissance variants of the Ju 88 entering service at that time, further development of the Do 215 B-2 was discontinued.

Do 215 B-3 was the designation assigned to two aircraft sold to the Soviet Union at the turn of 1939/40. They were bomber/reconnaissance machines powered by Daimler-Benz DB 601 Aa engines rated at 1,175 hp on take-off, and armed with three 7.92 mm MG 15 machine guns on flexible mounts. Both aircraft arrived in Moscow on 28th April 1940 at 15:32 hrs. They were despatched to the Central Aviation Research Institute, where test pilots Pavel F. Mushtayev and Mark L. Gallay, amongst others, flew them. Russian specialists were impressed with the ruggedness of the aircraft's construction. The Do 215

could easily land on one engine and was fitted with self-sealing fuel tanks. They were equally surprised by the versatility of the aircraft, the standardisation of its many elements and the simplicity of switching from bomber to reconnaissance variants, even under field conditions, by mounting an additional fuel tank in the bomb bay.

In the summer of 1941 the high command of the Soviet Air Force devised a plan to form a secret reconnaissance squadron equipped with, among other aircraft, the two Do 215 B-3s purchased in Germany. The unit was put under the command of Maj. Valentin I. Khomyakov, a seasoned veteran of the Spanish Civil War, and his deputy, a former test pilot Fiodor F. Opadczyy. Among the unit's flying personnel were several pro-communist Spanish pilots, who had

A very interesting Do 17 M-1 airframe at tests. Fuselage and control surfaces are covered with three-colour splinter camouflage, whilst the remaining surfaces of tail and wings are left in natural metal finish.

Dornier Do 17 M-1 undergoing landing gear retraction tests.

Dornier Do 17 M-1 with civil registration number at a factory airfield.

escaped to the Soviet Union after the Nationalists had won the Civil War. One of the two Do 215s was crewed by Antonio Arias and Vincente Beltram. However, the unit was not used operationally. The Do 215 B-4 was an improved reconnaissance version developed from the B-2, which saw service with 3. Aufklärungsstaffel des Oberkommandos der Luftwaffe.

Meanwhile, the shortage of night fighters forced the Luftwaffe high command to look for impromptu solutions. One of them was a decision to convert the last 20 Do 215 B-4 airframes into night fighters, designated Do 215 B-5. The onboard equipment was identical to the Do 17 Z-10 standard, with an IR searchlight for the

Spanner-Gerät infrared detection system. Do 215 B-5s were armed with four 7.92 mm MG 17 machine guns in the nose section, with a single 20 mm MG FF cannon mounted in a small gondola under the nose. At a later date several machines were upgunned with a single 7.92 mm MG 17 machine gun and three 20 mm MG FF cannons. The exhaust manifolds were fitted with flame dampers. The Do 215 B-5 had a crew of three, and its defensive armament consisted of two 7.92 mm MG 15 machine guns on flexible mounts, in the A– and B-Stand stations.

In the summer of 1941 a Do 215 B-5 of II./NJG 1, coded G9+OM, was fitted with a prototype

FuG (*Funk-Gerät*) 202 "Lichtenstein" airborne radar. In the summer of 1942 at Travemünde test station one Do 215 B-5 was experimentally armed with six to eight upward-firing 20 mm MG 151 cannons (the so-called *Schräge Musik* configuration). The *Spanner-Gerät* device, also directed upwards, was used for aiming, with the FuG 202 "Lichtenstein" radar used for target detection at a longer range.

Further development plans included a high-altitude, long-range reconnaissance version designated Do 215 B-6. It was to have a crew of four, three cameras and new Daimler-Benz DB 601 T engines with TK 9 A turbosuperchargers. Those powerplants, rated at 1,300 hp, were expected to give the aircraft a top speed of 480 kph at 9,000 metres.

The total production figure for all Dornier Do 215 variants was only 105 aircraft, all of them produced at the Dornier plant in Munich.

Operational service

In early 1937 Dornier Do 17 E-1s were allotted to I./KG 153 stationed at Merseburg and I./KG

Dornier Do 17 M-1 in RLM 70/71/65 finish, summer 1939.

Dornier Do 17 M-1 (coded GS+NR) powered by Bramo 323 A engines, of Luftdienst Gardemoen; Norway, July 1943.

Do 17 M-1's cockpit and instrument panel.

Dornier Do 17 P-2 prototype. Of note is the purpose-designed device for towing the aircraft attached to its tailwheel.

155 at Giebelstadt. At about the same time the first Do 17 F-1s were issued to Aufkl.Gr.(F)/122, a long-range reconnaissance unit based at Prenzlau, which by April 1937 was at its authorized strength of 36 aircraft. By the end of 1937 Do 17 E-1 bombers had also been delivered to II. and III./KG 153, as well as to II. and III./KG 155, which shared airfields at Finsterwalde and Altenburg. In October 1937, after KG 155 had entirely converted to the Do 17 E-1, the *Geschwader* was re-commissioned as KG 158. Before the month was out, IV./KG 153 was formed at Liegnitz (presently Legnica, Poland). It was to provide the nucleus for the newly-established KG 252. The following year IV./KG 153 was re-designated as II./KG 252. In November 1938, I./KG 252 was formed at Cottbus. By the end of 1938 a fourth *Kampfgeschwader* equipped with the Do 17 E-1 – KG 255 – began to take shape.

Throughout 1937 Do 17 E-1s equipped more long-range reconnaissance *Gruppen*:

Aufkl.Gr.(F)/121 at Neuhausen, Aufkl.Gr.(F)/123 at Großenhain, Aufkl.Gr.(F)/124 in Kassel, and Aufkl.Gr. 125 at Würzburg. Uffz. Friedrich Aufdemkamp was among the pilots who served with KG 255 'Alpengeschwader' during that period. He reported:

"When we returned to Landsberg, we saw the first Do 17s delivered to the Geschwader. I had heard so much good about this machine that I could barely wait to have a closer look at it. Yes, it was a beautiful aircraft, aerodynamically refined, with twin tailfins. The landing gear was operated hydraulically and looked reassuringly sturdy. The crew compartment housed three. From his seat the pilot had a nearly unlimited view all around him.

In mid-August 1937 I was checked out on the Do 17. I flew with Franz Vüllers to Lechfeld, which had a longer runway than the one we had at Landsberg. It was a safety precaution due to the Do 17's relatively high landing speed. How-

BMW 132 N radial engine, which powered Dornier Do 17 P.

Dornier do 17 P-1 viewed from the front.

ever, I had no problems whatsoever in mastering this beautiful and fast machine. After four bumps and circuits on my own my training was over (...).

By the summer KG 255 was fully equipped with Do 17s. Once I was tasked with test-flying a machine with a replaced engine. On that occasion I was accompanied by an engineer from an aircraft factory. Wishing to learn more about the aircraft's flight characteristics, I talked the engineer into performing several more air tests. I was advised to climb up to 3,000 meters and keep a straight course whilst changing engine revolutions. With the new powerplant satisfactorily tested, I proceeded to put the aircraft through its paces. First I reduced port engine revolutions, then switched it off and feathered the propeller. I maintained a straight course and, although I was now flying much slower, even on one engine the aircraft handled well. I even managed to gain some height. I was advised to turn starboard, i.e. the side with the engine on, but I managed to make a turn to port as well, although it demanded more caution. I repeated the whole procedure with the other engine turned off. Then, while flying straight, I began to reduce engine revolutions until the aircraft began to shudder and finally stalled. I put it into a dive, and when the hand of the airspeed gauge passed 400 kph, I pulled up into a climbing turn. I made several more chandelles, but looking at the faces of my companions I realized that they didn't enjoy this kind of flying. I promptly eased off for fear that they might involuntarily empty their stomachs. I passed Zugspitze[9], whereupon I throttled back and dived down the Höllental valley to Garmisch, before returning to Landsberg. A few days later I was confidentially told that the chief mechanic had been heard warning other ground crews: 'If you ever have to fly

Reconnaissance Dornier Do 17 P-1 coded U4+QH.

with Aufdemkamp, remember that he's a daredevil and a weirdo, who might get you killed!'

In the period between 1st and 13th September 1937 II./KG 255 moved to Giebelstadt near Würzburg. We were to join other units there for an air parade during the National Party Convention (*Reichsparteitag*).[10] We began to practice the expected tight formation of three-aircraft 'vics' during our transfer flight to the new airfield. It was easier said than done, however. Many pilots of our Gruppe had little experience. Since we were to fly one Staffel after another, it took time to form up. Such a tight formation was very demanding. Pilots had to watch carefully the neighbouring machines for fear of mid-air collisions. We trained intensely for the parade. At times my palms were wet with sweat from working on the yoke and throttles. Meanwhile my observer and radio operator, with little to do, were getting bored. For us, the pilots, however, it was hard work in the cockpit, sometimes two hours before noon and another two in the

Dornier Do 17 R-2, W.Nr. 2195 powered by DB 601 B engines, of Lichtbildsonderstaffel Rowehl, at a factory airfield.

One of first Dornier Do 17 Z-0s during factory trials.

The Do 17 Z-0 was fitted with a redesigned front section commonly known as the Waffenkopf.

Dornier Do 17 Z-0 in factory-applied splinter camouflage of RLM 70 Schwarzgrün and RLM 71 Dunkelgrün.

Ventral entry hatch in Dornier Do 17 Z-1.

afternoon, day after day. At first we practiced by Staffeln, then by Gruppen, and finally the entire Geschwader together (…).

13th September 1937 was the day of the air parade. Our huge formation assembled 50 km west of Nuremberg, and then headed straight for the rally grounds, flying at the altitude of 300-400 metres. Our show was quickly over, for we flashed past at 280-300 kph. We went back to our airfield, in a much more relaxed formation".[11]

Condor Legion

The first theatre of operations to see the Do 17 in combat was Spain, at that time embroiled in a bloody civil war. Both the German Condor Legion and the Spanish Nationalist air force deployed Ju 52/3m transports as improvised bombers. These slow, lumbering machines had to run the gauntlet of the relatively modern, Soviet-built Polikarpov I-15 and I-16 fighters used by the Republicans. In December 1936 Hptm. Rudolf Freiherr von Moreau, one of the Condor Legion's

Assembly hall with Dornier Do 17 Z-2s' fuselages.

Construction details of Dornier Do 17 Z's rear fuselage.

Do 17 Z's engine nacelles being assembled.

most distinguished pilots, was summoned to Berlin to report to the Luftwaffe's commander-in-chief on the situation in Spain. After the briefing Herman Göring resolved to form and despatch to Spain an experimental bomber squadron (*Versuchsbomberstaffel*) equipped with the then latest German bomber types: four Ju 86 D-1s, four He 111 B-1s, and four Do 17 E-1s. The four Do 17s[12] arrived in Spain in February 1937. There they joined VB/88, a new bomber unit, and were coded 27•1 through 27•4. The Do 17 was nicknamed 'Bacalao' (Codfish) by the Spanish.

The Do 17s debuted in combat on 12th March 1937. On 20th March 1937, operating from Matacán-Salamanca airfield, they raided the positions of Republican troops in Barajas and Alcalá de Henares areas. They were very active on 25th March 1937 bombing the town of Ocana, and later that day Aranjuez railway station and a nearby steel railway bridge, which was knocked out.

In late March 1937 VB/88 relocated to Burgos to assist in Gen. Franco's offensive against Bilbao. At 09:00 hrs on 31st March 1937 the Do 17s bombed enemy positions near Ochandiano. The following day six bombers (one He 111, two Ju 86s and three Do 17s) dropped a total of five tons of bombs. On 2nd April, while the Nationalists stormed the second line of Republican defences at Mecoleta, the same six bombers dropped eight and a half tons of bombs.

The following days brought along deteriorating weather conditions, which considerably curtailed air operations. Do 17s flew singly, attempting to bomb their assigned tar-

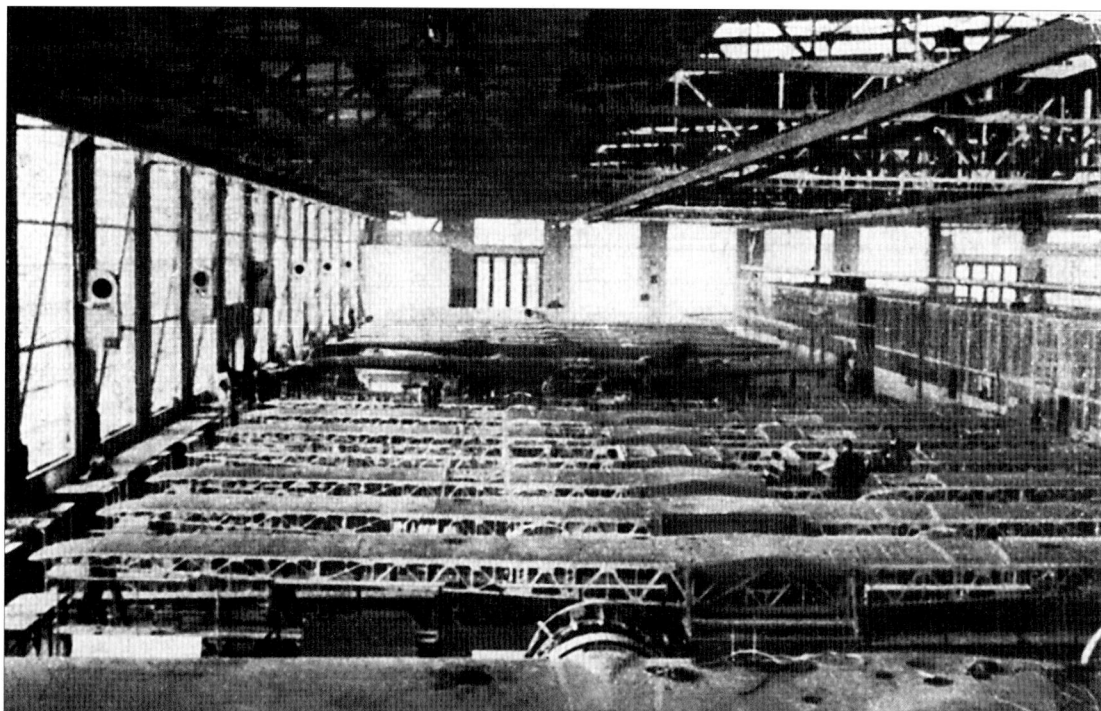

Do 17 Z's wings assembled in Dornier plant.

Do 17 Z's wing on a trolley. Note construction details of flaps and main landing gear wheel wells.

Dornier Do 17 Z-1 crashed in a forced landing.

Dornier Do 17 Z-2 of I./KG 2 photographed during the Balkan campaign at Plovdiv airfield, Bulgaria, April 1941.

gets despite the low cloud deck. During one of these missions Felipe del Rio Crespo[13], the top-scoring Republican fighter pilot of the so-called northern front, shot down a Do 17 E-1 coded 27•2 whilst flying a Soviet-built I-15 bi-plane fighter. Two members of the crew (Uffz. Otto Hoffmeister and Uffz. Friedriech Müller) were killed when they fell into the river before their parachutes had fully opened. The pilot, Oblt. Hans Sobotka, went down with his aircraft. A crowd gathered at the crash site, which was located in the middle of an open, heather-covered field, and stared at the flaming wreck and the body of the pilot, which had

Dornier Do 17 Z-1's instrument panel.

been thrown clear. Sobotka was lying on his back, partly-burned, his body twisted. His arms were crossed in front of his face[14].

On the afternoon of 22nd April 1937 the Do 17s bombed Bilbao aerodrome. Four days later, on 26th April, a single Do 17 dropped bombs near Renteria bridge at the village of Guernica, marking the target for the main K/88 force. Most of the bombs hit residential areas, killing nearly 300 civilians.[15]

On 7 May 1937 three Do 17s, escorted by seven Bf 109s, bombed a Republican airfield in Santander. The attack was unsuccessful and had to be repeated the following day. By the end of May 1937 the Do 17s of VB/88 had mounted five more raids, mainly against Amorebieta. On 19th

Dornier Do 17 Z-3 of KGr. 606 at Cherbourg airfield, France, summer 1940.

Close-up of KGr. 606 emblem painted in the fuselage front section of the unit's Dornier Do 17 Zs.

Dornier Do 17 Z-0, D-AIIB, was rebuilt as Do 215 V1 prototype. Note unusual, 'export' camouflage on the upper surfaces. (This and next two photos)

fensive to alleviate the pressure being exerted by the Nationalists on Madrid. On 24th July 1937 VB/88 lost its second Do 17 E-1, coded 27•5. Its crew bailed out. With more He 111s arriving from Germany, in mid-August 1937 the Condor Legion HQ decided to pass all the available Do 17s to A/88, the reconnaissance squadron, which at that time was stationed at Villarcayo. A/88 lost its first Dornier (27•11) on 15th August 1937 in a take-off crash (the crew was unhurt).

In early October 1937 A/88 moved to Santander, where it operated over the central and northern fronts. The turn of December 1937 and January 1938 saw a ferocious battle at Teruel. Besides their usual reconnaissance missions, Do 17s of A/88 were pressed into service as bombers. In the period between 27th December 1937 and 6th January 1938 they dropped four tons of bombs daily. On 10th January 1938, near a road junction north of Teruel, one of the Dorniers was hit by anti-aircraft fire, but managed to limp back to base. On 13th January Do 17s targeted Venta del Puente, and on 16th-17th January Villed and Guadalajara. Until the end of January 1938 the Do 17s were very active against enemy troop concentrations.

On 5th February 1938 a curious incident occurred. A bomb dropped only seconds earlier from Do 17 E-1 27•1 suddenly exploded, badly damaging the aircraft. Two crew members, the commander of A/88, Hptm. Gerndt and Ogefr. Meix both suffered injuries. The Dornier limped back home. It was later determined that the bomb had most probably been struck by an anti-aircraft round moments after it had left the bomb bay. That chance hit turned out to be a lesser evil for the Dornier's crew, for a direct strike in the aircraft's belly would have caused much more extensive damage and very likely brought down the bomber. The injured Hptm. Gerndt was replaced by Hptm. Hentschel at the head of A/88.

In the weeks to come the Do 17s continued in their dual role of reconnaissance machines and bombers, performing pinpoint attacks against railway stations, transport columns, ammunition dumps and major road intersections.

June 1937 Bilbao was captured by Gen. Franco's troops.

At the turn of June and July 1937 eight more Do 17s, coded 27•5 through 27•12, were delivered to Spain[16]. Hence, at least four machines could be transferred to the reconnaissance unit (A/88). In early July 1937 VB/88 relocated to Salamanca, where it shared the airfield with bombers of K/88. In the ensuing weeks the Germans focused their efforts on the Brunete area, where the Republican forces had launched a counterof-

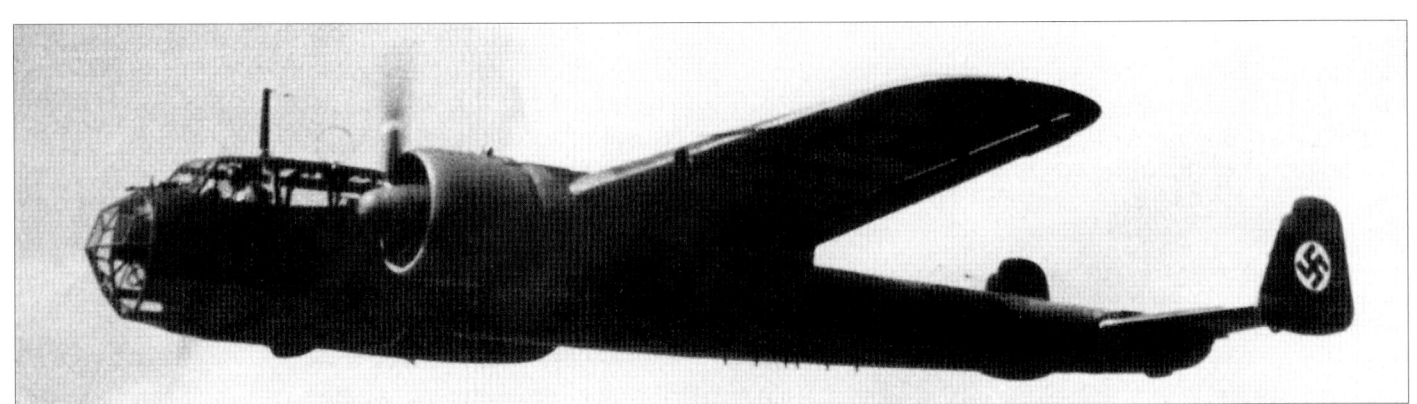

On 9th March 1938 the Nationalists launched another offensive, strongly supported from the air by the Condor Legion. On 10th March Do 17s of A/88 bombed Bujaraloz and a railway station at Escatrón, where a train carrying members of the Republican air force general staff had stopped. The following day the Dorniers flew seven reconnaissance missions along the Ebro river. More days packed with intense air activity ensued. On 13th March the Do 17s raided Montalbán, Alcañiz and Caspe, on the 14th Bujaraloz, on the 15th Ebre, and on the 17th La Zaida and Escatrón.

During the second phase of the Nationalist offensive, Arascues came under attack on 22nd March, whilst Granen, Sesa and the Sarinena railway line were visited on the 24th. On 25th March the Do 17s reconnoitred roads east of Saragossa and Huesca, on the 26th the Albalete area, and on the 27th roads from Frega to Monzón, as well as fortifications around Monzón. The following day, 28th March, the Do 17s bombed the intersections of roads connecting Monzón, Frega and Lérida. Interdiction operations were continued on 29th March with attacks on the road intersections between the Cinga and Segre rivers. A/88's

This Dornier Do 17 Z-0 served as an airborne dynamometer platform for ramjet engines.

involvement in supporting the Nationalist ground forces continued unabated during the first ten days of April 1938. On the 7th day of the month A/88 was dealt a disheartening loss. Over Cubelles an anti-aircraft round scored a direct hit on one of the Do 17s, which crashed in flames three kilometres south-west of Artesa. Its entire crew – Lt. Max Kendel, Uffz. Paul Birkhofen, Uffz. Willi von der Driesch and Ogefr. Erich Fiedler – perished.

Close-up of fuselage front section and DB 601 A-1 engine, which powered the Dornier Do 215 B-1.

Dornier Do 17 F-1 transferred from 1.A/88 of the Condor Legion to Spanish Gruppo 8-G-27 in August 1937, the badge of the German unit is visible on the engine cowling. The aircraft sports RLM 70/71/65 paint scheme.

Do 215 V3, 25+C03 powered by 1,100 hp Daimler-Benz DB 601 A engines. Of note are code markings painted on wing uppersurafaces. This head-on view offers a good look at the extensively glazed nose section, known as the "Waffenkopf", of Do 215 V3.

Dornier Do 215 B-1 coded NO+TB passing over the Alps during test flights.(Photos on this and next page)

In early May 1938 the Do 17s of A/88 were stationed at Buñuel and Tauste. Shortly afterwards the unit relocated to Vinaroz. On 18th May the Do 17s bombed Cabanes, Oroposa and Benicasim: between the 23rd and 26th they raided Lucena del Cid and Vistabella directly behind the frontlines, as well as Castellón and Al-manzora located in the rear areas. On 28th May, during four separate missions, they hit Ares de Maestre and Castellón railway station. During the weeks that followed the Do 17s were busy paving the way for the Nationalists advancing towards Valencia. In mid-July A/88 passed five of its Dorniers (27•3, •13, •17, •19 and •21)

to its Spanish allies, and received nine factory-fresh machines from Germany.

Meanwhile, on the night of 25th July 1938 the Republicans launched their last offensive of the war, attacking across the Ebro River and initially gaining some ground. The Condor Legion, which usually served as Gen. Franco's airborne 'fire brigade' was immediately deployed at the battlefield. The Do 17s, beside their regular reconnaissance duties, flew as many as four bomber missions daily. On 5th August 1938 the unit suffered another operational loss. Over Felix, Republican anti-aircraft batteries knocked down the Do 17 F-1 coded 27•16. Uffz. Otto Lehmann was killed, whereas Oblt. Wolf Fach and Ofw. Friedrich Mende bailed out and were captured.

The fast pace of operations combined with notorious shortages of spare parts – especially tail wheel tyres, which were quickly worn out on the rugged runways – took a heavy toll on the Do 17s' serviceability. By mid-August 1938 A/88 was reduced to only four airworthy Do 17s. In that period the unit's activity was limited to reconnaissance sorties, which were carried out in parallel with missions flown by 8-G-27, a Spanish squadron also equipped with Do 17s.

On 1st September 1938 the crew of Do 17 F-1, coded 27•25, brushed with death when a 37 mm anti-aircraft shell embedded itself in the aircraft's port wing without exploding. Nevertheless, the damage caused by the impact was so extensive that the machine was taken off operations for several months. Also in September 1938, at Llanes airfield, Do 17 27•26 was written off in a failed belly landing.

After the Battle of the Ebro, on 17th November 1938 A/88 was stood down. Of nine Do 17s on the unit's strength, one serviceable machine was all that could be mustered. Things changed for the better only after several weeks of badly needed rest had passed, and with the arrival of a few of the latest Do 17 P-1s (one of them was passed to the Spanish 8-G-27). On 8th December 1938 A/88 was back on operations, this time in the province of Catalonia. As of 23rd December 1938 the unit, stationed at Benuel, could field 11 Do 17s. The following month Maj. Matussek assumed command. In late February 1939 three Dorniers (27•4, •9 and •18) were handed over to the Spaniards of 8-G-27. At that time A/88 had only three airworthy Do 17s (two E-1s and one Do 17 P-1) on strength, stationed at Sanjuro-Saragossa, with

Dornier Do 215 B-1 with dismantled front machine guns.

Dornier Do 215 B-4 (PK+FO) undergoing flight test.

two more Dorniers under repair in León. With the fall of Madrid on 28th March 1939 the Spanish Civil War was practically over.

The most distinguished Do 17 crew to have seen action in Spain was Ofw. Ernst Sorge (pilot), Lt. Philips and Uffz. Wawrock, who flew 57 operational sorties. The Dornier Do 17 had proved its worth as a long-range reconnaissance machine. Neither Spanish nor even Italian aircraft could match its performance. Furthermore, bomb raids carried out by single Do 17s were performed with high accuracy, which compensated for the aircraft's modest payload. After the end of hostilities the surviving 12 Do 17s were handed over to the Spanish Air Force.

Blitzkrieg in Poland

The German Air Force's primary task in the war against Poland was to win air supremacy. Once this was accomplished, the Luftwaffe could concentrate on close support of its ground and naval forces. However, heavy clouds and morning mists foiled the Germans' detailed schedule of air attacks for 1st September 1939, the first day of the war, and the Luftwaffe did not fulfil most of its assigned tasks. The main strikes against the bases of the Polish Air Force were delayed until the afternoon.

KG 2 was put on combat alert well before daybreak, at 02:00 hrs. At 04:45 hrs 30 Do 17 Zs and two Do 17 Us took off from Schippen-

Another machine of the same production run bearing Stammkenzeichen PK+EM.

Camouflage pattern covering the upper surfaces of this Dornier Do 215 B-4 is shown here to advantage.

Dornier Do 215 B-4 (W.Nr. 40, coded PK+FH) at a factory airfield.

Snow-capped Dornier Do 17 E-1 at Burg aerodrome, at the turn of 1938/39. Visible in the background is Junkers Ju 87 dive bomber of St.G 77.

beil for the first combat mission. Maintaining a tight formation at 5,000 metres, the bombers approached their target at about 06:00 hrs: an aerodrome at Terespol/Małaszewicze. Suddenly, one of the Dorniers was caught in the slipstream of the machine flying ahead of it and snapped into a spin. Before the pilot, Uffz. Franz Schmidt of 4./KG 2, could regain control of the aircraft its flight engineer, Fw. Wilhelm Holewa – a veteran of the Condor Legion – panicked and bailed out, forgetting to fasten his parachute. It was the unit's first fatality, an accidental and senseless non-combat loss. Uffz. Schmidt managed to pull his aircraft out of the spin and join the formation in time for the bomb drop. Seven hangars were claimed destroyed at the airfield, along with nine twin-engined machines hit on the ground. Polish sources acknowledged the loss of six 'Łoś' and four 'Żubr' bombers, as well as four Fokker transports.

During the return flight, over the city of Łomża Polish anti-aircraft artillery hit the Do 17 Z of 6./KG 2 flown by Lt. Hans Wilhelm Tamm. The aircraft began to quickly lose fuel and was forced to belly-in behind enemy lines, some ten kilometres north-west of Brodnica. Lt. Tamm and Oblt. Rudi Westhaus evaded capture, and

on 3rd September encountered forward German troops. Meanwhile Ofw. Walter Seese and Uffz. Rudolf Hängsgen were taken prisoner and remained in Polish captivity until the Russians freed them on 29th September.

At 05:15 hrs 32 Do 17 Ms took off from Gerdauen to strike at Grodno aerodrome. The aircraft also strafed a train encountered on the Grodno – Augustów line. By 08:01 hrs all the machines had returned safely to base. In the afternoon I./KG 2 bombed an airfield at Płock, whilst II./KG 2 struck off for an airfield at Lida, where at least four aircraft and three fuel tanks were burned.

The Do 17 Zs of II./KG 3 started their campaign against Poland at 04:26 hrs, taking off from Heiligenbeil. They targeted the airfields at Kutno and Grudziądz, the army barracks at Płock, and freight trains on the Toruń – Kutno railway line. Two bombers were damaged by

Reconnaissance Dornier Do 17 F-1 coded 27•7 of Condor Legion's A/88 in Spain.

Dornier Do 17 E-1, coded 27•25, of A/88. Noteworthy are emblems painted on front section of the fuselage and engine cowlings.

SC 50 bomb about to be loaded. In the background a Do 17 E of A/88, Condor Legion.

Dornier Do 17 E-1s of 7./KG 255 'Alpen'. The unit's emblem, the Edelweiss, is clearly visible.

ground fire. Oblt. Walter Schott of 4./KG 2 was killed onboard one of them, and two other crew members were injured. Fw. Gerhard Schneider of 6./KG 2 suffered injuries.

In the afternoon II./KG 2 set out to strike ammunition dumps near Grudziądz and a troop concentration near Jabłonowo railway station. An airfield at Grudziądz was also strafed. Polish ack-ack guns brought down one Do 17 Z, which crash-landed behind the lines near Książki (Hohenkirch). Uffz. Heinz Steinbeitz perished in the crash; the remaining crew members were hidden from the Poles by local ethnic Germans (the *Volksdeutsche*) until the ar-

rival of Wehrmacht troops. Another Do 17 Z, a machine of 4./KG 3 coded 5K+EM and flown by Uffz. Erich Beyer, returned to base with 23 shrapnel holes. In an overlapping action III./KG 3 bombed the army barracks at Tczew. Several aircraft were slightly damaged by anti-aircraft fire.

Meanwhile, due to inclement weather conditions, the first mission of I./KG 76, which operated from Breslau-Schöngarden, was scrapped shortly after take-off and the bombers were ordered to return to base. Nevertheless, a dozen or so machines pressed on; 2./76 bombed an airfield at Radom, destroying four aircraft and

airfield facilities, whereas four Do 17 Zs of 3./ KG 76 attacked Opoczno railway station. Concurrently III./KG 76 despatched 33 aircraft to knock out an airfield at Skierniewice, but in marginal weather only 9./KG 76 located the target, destroying three hangars and other ground facilities. One flight from 8./KG 76 hit barracks at Tomaszów, another an airfield in Łódź. Other aircraft returned to base with full bombload.

In the afternoon 28 Dorniers went after airfields in Częstochowa, Kielce and Radom. Marshalling yards and railway stations located along the Kielce – Chorzów line were also targeted. Of all the Do 17 units which saw action on 1st September 1939, KG 77 registered the highest losses – seven machines. In the morning the *Geschwader* was up in force, directing

110 of its Do 17 Es against Kraków-Rakowice airbase, where some 40 Polish aircraft were destroyed on the ground. The loss of two Do 17 Es of 7./KG 77 has remained a disputed issue ever since. According to Polish historians[17] both Dorniers were shot down by ppor. (2/Lt) Władysław Gnyś. However, German historian Marius Emmerling, having analysed German reports, concluded that the two Dorniers had collided after one of them had been hit by anti-aircraft fire. Hans Höchersteiger of 7./KG 77 reminisced:

"At 05:00 hrs we took off for an attack against Kraków airbase in Poland. The closer we were to the Polish-German border, the more of our troops we saw on the roads. Then we ventured into the hostile airspace. This was

Dornier Do 17 E-1s of 4./KG 155 passing over central Germany, 1938. The aicraft in the foreground is coded 53 + B24.

Bombing of Warsaw photographed from a Do 17P. Dorniers preparing for the bomb release are marked by white circles. The other photo shows the results of the bombing.

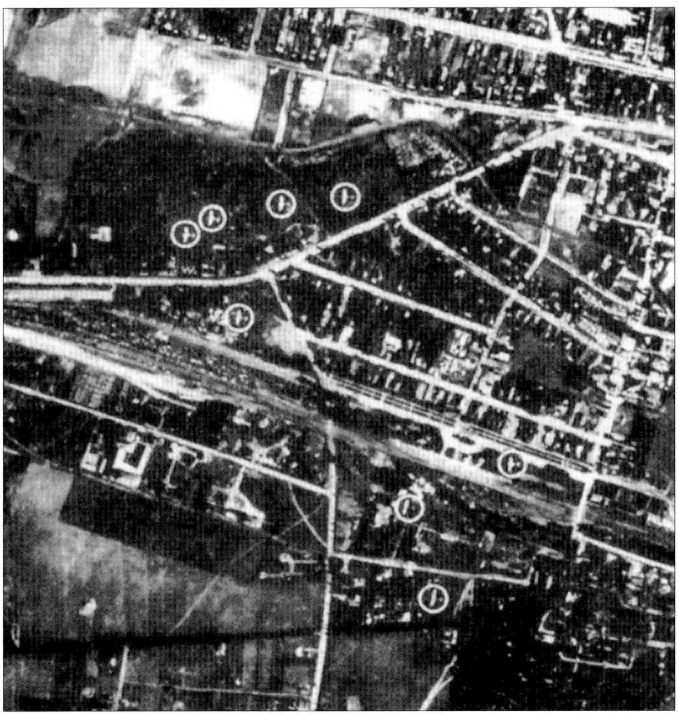

Do 17E and Do 17P of the 121st Long Range Reconnaissance Squadron, Olsztyn (Allenstein) 1939.

Do 17 at an airfield in Slovakia, 1939.

Close-up of the nose of the Do 17 P-1 reconnaissance version in three-color camouflage.

Dornier Do 17 P-1 reconnaissance aircraft damaged by Polish anti-aircraft artillery.

our first combat mission. We anxiously awaited the enemy reaction... Ground fire! One of our flights came under fire from Polish anti-aircraft guns. The leading machine of the 'vic' swerved to port and crashed into the left Kettenhund[18]. In one instant our Staffel lost six comrades. None of the two Do 17s was lost to Polish fighters. It was a result of ground fire (light Flak or anti-aircraft machine guns). This was what we were told upon landing by the crew of the third aircraft in that flight. None of us actually witnessed the collision".[19]

On the second day of the war Do 17s continued to raid Polish airfields, marshalling yards and troop concentrations. II./KG 2 bombed an airfield at Małaszewicze, whilst I./KG 2 for the first time directly supported ground operations, hitting enemy troops and supply columns in the Grodno – Augustów – Suwałki area. In the afternoon I./KG 2 delivered heavy strikes against airfields at Lida and Vilnius. On Sunday, 3rd September 1939, KG 2 was ordered to bomb Polish fortifications near the town of Mława, braving intense and accurate anti-aircraft fire. Nine Do 17s were damaged and one shot down

The most important equipment of the Do 17 P-1 reconnaissance aircraft were Rb 10/18, Rb 20/30 and Rb 50/30 photo cameras.

Dornier Do 17 P-1 at a factory airfield, prior to being delivered to an operational unit. Of note is the aircraft's serial number, W.Nr. 4013, scribbled with chalk on the upper tailfin.

The nose of the Dornier Do 17 P-1, 4U+LL of 3.(F)/123 with a bar symbolizing an aerial victory scored over Poland on 8 September 1939.

Dornier Do 17 E-1 coded 3Z+DA of Stab KG 77, summer 1939.

(its commander, Oblt. Rudolf Krochmann, was killed). On Monday, 4th September 1939, Dorniers of III./KG 3 set upon a column of the Polish 70th and 29th Infantry Regiments retreating along the roads between the towns of Turek and Uniejów. Attacking at low level, the Germans came under unexpectedly accurate anti-aircraft fire. No fewer than eight Do 17s were either shot down or forced to belly-land; three crewmembers were killed, and a further 14 suffered injuries. This turned out to be the greatest single success of the Polish anti-aircraft defences against the Luftwaffe throughout the entire campaign.

Do 17s continued to render close air-support to the advancing German troops until the

A Do 17E at a provisional airfield in Sudetenland.

end of the campaign in Poland. Once the Polish army was defeated in the field, most bomb raids were directed against the besieged Modlin fortress and the city of Warsaw. Overall, 38 Do 17s of all versions were lost over Poland. Of those, 11 were written off in crashes, 25 fell to AA guns, and two to fighters.[20]

Campaign in the West

As in Poland in September 1939, when the German invasion of France and the Low Countries was launched (codenamed operation "Fall Gelb") Do 17s formed part of the force tasked with neutralizing Allied airfields, communication centres, supply lines and troop concentrations.[21]

In the late afternoon of 9th May 1940 the component *Gruppen* of KG 2 were put on combat alert. Shortly after midnight, duty officers shouting, 'Briefing in ten minutes' roused the flying personnel from their sleep. Crews of 1. and 2./ KG 2 were briefed to bomb Reims-Champagne airfield. Take-off time was set at 03:45 hrs:

"The day broke shortly after take-off, which had taken place in the pre-dawn darkness lit

Dornier Do 17 P-1 of a weather reconnaissance squadron in 1939. The aircraft sports RLM 70/71/65 paint scheme.

Do 17 E-1s and Zs of KG 77, photographed in August 1939. In the foreground 3Z+LM of 4. Staffel.

Rear gunner's station on Do 17 M-1 was armed with a single 7.92 mm MG 15 machine gun.

only by stars. Banks of mist hanging low above the ground made navigation extremely difficult. After 90 minutes of flight, suddenly a French airfield emerged below. It was too late to release our bombs. We had to turn around and approach the target again. Meanwhile the drone of our engines alerted the French on the ground. Our bombers were greeted with a formidable fusillade of anti-aircraft fire, which hit the machine of our Gruppenkommandeur. Major Martin Gutzmann was injured. Despite the Flak barrage our crews pressed on, dropping bombs on targets visible below. Numerous bursts were seen among hangars and across the landing ground. The French I. and II./15 bomber groups and the British No 226 Sqn each lost several aircraft destroyed on the ground.

At about 05:30 hrs machines of 3./KG 2 took off, making for the enemy airfields at Stenay, located between Sedan and Verdun. The German bombers encountered no opposition and after accomplishing their mission they returned

Dornier Do 17 E-1 damaged in a n emergency landing. Unit's emblem, painted in the front section of the fuselage, was censored out.

Among the Luftwaffe bombers which participated in the campaign in Poland in September 1939 were Do 17 Z-1s of KG 77.

Dornier Do 17 Z-1 (coded 3Z+BM) of 4./KG 77; Poland, September 1939.

Dornier Do 17 Z-1s undergo preflight maintenance, September 1939.

A crash-landed Dornier Do 17 P-1 of an unidentified reconnaissance unit; Poland, September 1939.

safely to base. At 04:56 hrs 4./KG 2 scrambled from Ansbach. They were bound for Yutz airfield near Diedenhofen (Thionville). In the target area the Staffel, flying at 5,700 metres, was jumped by enemy fighters. Four Do 17s, damaged by gunfire, dropped out of formation. The crew commanded by Uffz. Schiwek, flying on the right side of the rearmost flight, was engaged by fighters four consecutive times. During one of their firing passes the locking mechanism of the ventral entry hatch was knocked out, and flight engineer Fw. Ottlik fell out of the aircraft. He was most fortunate to have his parachute on. Immediately upon landing he was taken prisoner by the French.

During the fourth attack one engine of Uffz. Schiwek's Do 17 caught fire. The aircraft dropped out of formation and turned for friendly territory. It was badly shot-up and could no longer stay aloft. When the other engine seized up, the pilot belly-landed at Oberesch near Merzig in Saarland, just inside the German border with France.

Fw. Schmid's crew, which flew on the left flank of the rearmost flight, was less fortunate. Knocked out of the formation by fighters, their aircraft was immediately forced to crash-land and was captured by the French. Also Uffz. Veit's machine was also attacked by fighters, which knocked out one of its engines. Veit nursed his

failing aircraft back as far Katzweiler near Kaiser-slautern, where he made an emergency landing.

A fourth Do 17 was shot down, its crew left with no option but to 'hit the silk'. Observer Uffz. Strüven's parachute got entangled with the aircraft's antenna mast, and he was dragged to his death by the falling machine. The remaining crewmembers were taken prisoner.

Meanwhile 5./KG 2 went after an airfield at Chatel-Chéhéry. At 05:10 hrs, while crossing the Franco-Luxemburg frontier near Esch, the Staffel was bounced by fighters. In the ensuing shootout one German airman was killed, and another injured. However, the Do 17s accomplished their task and returned to base without further losses.

Dornier Do 17 M-1 (coded A5+BA) of Stab St.G 1, autumn 1939.

Long-range reconnaissance Dornier Do 17 P-1 (coded U4+QH); Germany, autumn 1939. Of interest are oversized crosses on wing upper surfaces. In the background a Messerschmitt Bf 109 E-1 sporting markings of I. Gruppe commander.

Dornier Do 17 P-1, B-4+FA, in RLM 70/71/65 finish. Construction details of flaps are demonstrated here to advantage. Of further interest is the location of the swastika, which suggests that the airframe was manufactured before June 1939.

6./KG 2 also had to fight their way through the enemy fighter screen. In a scrap in the Reims-Mourmelon area Uffz. Heinrich's machine was shot down; the entire crew perished. Of Uffz. Birkner's crew only the pilot and flight engineer, Uffz. Volz, managed to save their lives by taking to their parachutes (both were captured).

The bomber crews fought back with determination, and their concentrated return fire proved costly for the interceptors. French Lieutenant Roy had to break off the attack with injuries to his face and a smashed canopy. Lieutenant Goupy was shot in his thigh, and was fortunate

to bring his fighter down for an emergency landing before he passed out in the cockpit due to loss of blood. Overall, pilots of the French GC I./5 fighter group equipped with Curtiss fighters (Capt. Accart, Capt. Bouvard, Lts. Roy and Goupy, and Sgt. Perina) claimed two Do 17s shot down.

In an overlapping action III./KG 2 headed for airfields at Mourmelon (7. and 8. Staffeln) and Challerange (9. Staffel). Take-off time from Illesheim was set at 04:25 hrs. Over Thionville 9./KG 2 lost one of its crewmembers under somewhat puzzling circumstances. At about 05:10 hrs a crewman fell out of the ventral C-

Long-range reconnaissance Dornier Do 17 P-1 on the western front, late autumn 1939. Of interest is the emblem – a fox caring away a geese with a Gallic girl chasing it and Chamberlain.

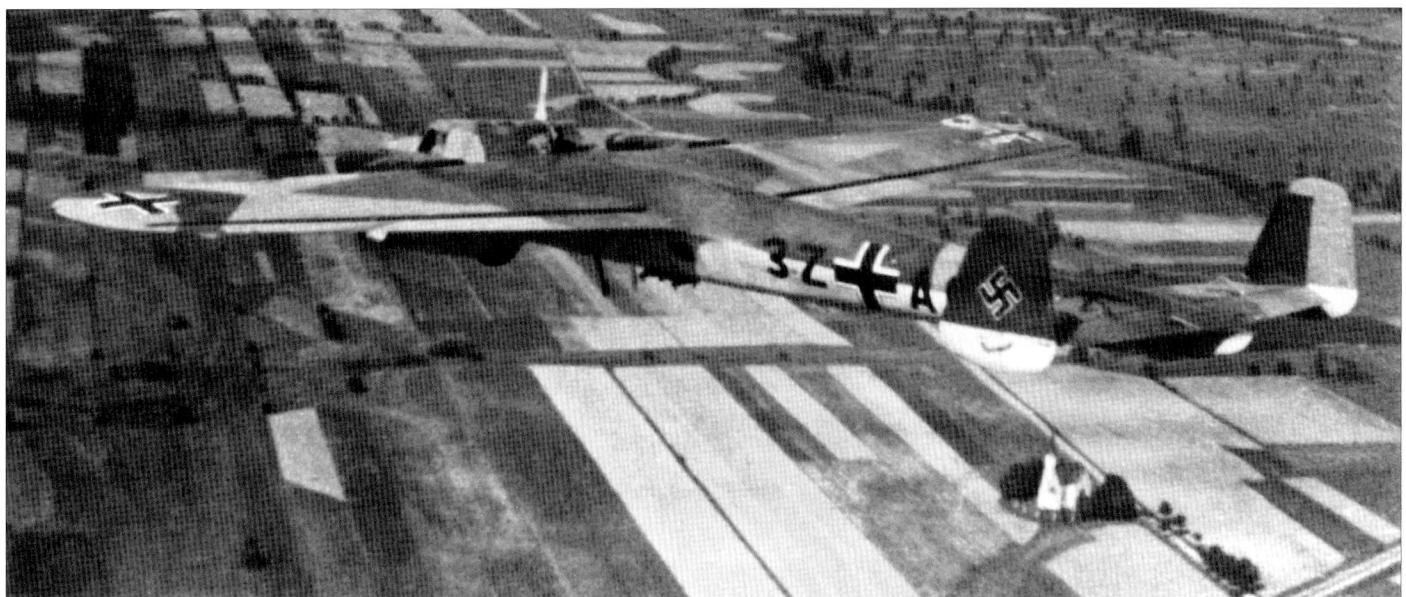

Stand gunner station. For a couple of seconds he desperately clutched at the rim of the hatch, then fell free from a height of 4,500 metres. Fortunately, he was seen to pull the ripcord of his parachute. Fw. Glanz, a flight engineer, ended up in French captivity.

Only light AA fire was encountered in the target area. At Mourmelon – at the receiving end – was No 88 Sqn RAF equipped with Fairey Battle light bombers. The Do 17s of 7./KG 2 came off the bomb run in a wide orbit to port and headed east. South of Camp de Chalons a French fighter bounced one of the Dorniers, which had straggled behind the formation. The German pilot, Lt. Krieger, got away with one shot-up engine, bringing his bomber down for a belly landing near Kaiserslautern".[22]

On the afternoon of 10th May 1940, and in the morning of the following day, Do 17s continued to harass French airfields. The most successful attack was mounted by nine Do 17 Zs of 4./KG 2 led by Oblt. Reimers. The German bombers flashed over the Maginot Line at a height of only a couple of dozen metres and arrived at Vraux airfield, where Blenheims of No 114 Sqn RAF were stationed. The British bombers, which were just taxiing out, were caught flat-footed. Nine of them were destroyed and the rest damaged in a hail of German bombs, followed by strafing attacks. Upon completion of this raid one Do 17 Z, coded U5+GM and flown by Lt. Bornschein, circled the field – which by that time had many burning wrecks strewn across it. Ofw. Borner, Lt. Bornschein's radio operator,

Dornier Do 17 E-1 of Stab II./ KG 77, autumn 1939. The aircraft carries a tri-colour camouflage on wing upper surfaces, composed of RLM 61 Dunkelbraun, RLM 62 Grün and RLM 63 Hellgrau.

A Do 17Z-2 of KG 2 carefully camouflaged with nets at Arras airfield.

recorded the scene on his camera. The film, when passed to the headquarters of the II. Fliegerkorps commander, duly impressed Gen. Lt. Loerzer.

On their return flight the Do 17 Z coded U5+LM collided with a tree. As the bomber limped along, enemy anti-aircraft gunners zeroed in on the cripple. The pilot, *Staffelkapitän* Oblt. Reimers was injured. His observer, Ofw. Krüger, took over the controls and managed to fly the aircraft to Frankfurt-Rebstock aero-

drome, where he bellied in. At the same time 9./KG 2 bombed Ecury-sur-Coole airfield, which housed No 150 Sqn RAF, a Fairey Battle outfit. This time the Germans missed the opportunity to knock out their enemy on the ground. Only one Battle was destroyed as a result of this attack, and another damaged.

On 13th May 1940 the focal point of Do 17s' operations shifted to Allied troop concentrations at the approaches to Sedan. In early evening III./KG 2 was directed against targets around

An interesting shot of a reconnaissance Dornier Do 17 P-1 demonstrating camouflage pattern on the aircraft's upper surfaces; western front, winter 1939.

Dornier Do 17 P-1, 4U+DL of 3.(F)/123 in pre-war RLM 61/62/63/65, but with national insignia of the new type, spring of 1940.

This reconnaissance Dornier Do 17 P-1 coded Z5+?? was shot down on the western front in spring 1940.

Dornier Do 17 Z-2 of 3./KG 76, spring 1940. Note unit's emblem under cockpit.

the town of Charleville. There the Dorniers were greeted with heavy and accurate anti-aircraft fire. Six crewmembers were injured. Ofw. Chill, one of the pilots, succumbed to his wounds in a Luftwaffe field hospital on the same day. One machine of 7./KG 2 (flown by Fw. Klöttchen) was shot down and its crew made PoWs. Two more, including the aircraft flown by the *Staffelkapitän* of 9./KG 2 Oblt. Davids, were seriously damaged and forced to crash-land at Biblis airfield. Lt. Bechtle of 9./KG 2, who participated in this raid, recalled:

"To the right we can see Mezieres, a few factory chimneys and a pall of smoke, which unmistakably marks a freshly bombed area. This must be the marshalling yards, the target assigned to our 8. Staffel. We are rapidly descending towards the ground. The bomb bay doors are already open. We race to the southwest, towards the road to Chalons and Rethel. With barely 20 metres separating us from the ground, we are hedgehopping along. We have to maintain visual contact with our flight leader. My flight is led by Oblt. Davids, flying to the right

This Dornier Do 17 Z-2 of KG 3 suffered combat damage during campaign in the West in May 1940.

Dornier Do 17 Z-2 of KG 76 on a combat sortie over France, May 1940.

Dornier Do 17 Z-2 z KG 77 photographed during the campaign in the West, in May 1940.

Close-up of Dornier Do 17 Z-2's front section, demonstrating its enhanced armament of seven 7.92 mm MG 15 machine guns on flexible mounts.

Dornier Do 17 Z-2 of Stab ZG 26, western front, summer 1940.

Dornier Do 17 Z-1 being readied for a combat sortie.

and ahead of my machine. Then we run into columns of French troops, trucks and horse-drawn carts. These images are etched in my memory as if they were recorded on a film. The French below us scatter, seeking shelter under trees and in ditches running on either side of the road, many vehicles burn. Roads leading out of the towns are jammed with traffic.

Enemy columns marching north spread out to adjacent roads, and there run head-on into the endless stream of refugees heading in the opposite direction. Their belongings are piled up on trolleys pushed by women and children, colourful bedding clearly standing out in the distance. Livestock are wandering amongst the people. Under my strict orders my flight engi-

RAF personnel carries a part of the fuselage of a downed Do-17Z-2 of KG 2, August 1940.

neer and observer fire their machine guns only at soldiers. So far, we had not found a target worthy of our bombs.

Suddenly, at the edge of a nearby town, I notice a partially camouflaged concentration of vehicles. I climb up and point out the target to my observer. At the same instant the air is filled with dust and debris thrown up by the explosions of bombs dropped by a flight ahead of us. I will always remember those heavy logs swirling like a handful of matches tossed in the air. Only by violently skidding to one side did I manage to avoid a seemingly imminent collision with the whirling mess. I instinctively hunch down in the cockpit for fear that one of those logs will crash into us.

From the corner of my right eye I constantly check on my leader's machine in order to maintain our 'vic' formation. I can see his port engine, which must have been hit from the ground, begin to belch dark smoke. The stricken aircraft falls back and starts to claw for altitude. The propeller of the damaged engine comes to a halt. Oblt. Reiss, the other wingman flying on the right flank, and I both throttle back to keep our station behind the leader. Our commander turns to starboard, the side with the functioning engine, making for home base. He waves the two of us away.

Now we are on our own. I make a wide curve to the northwest, looking for something to hide me from the enemy. To the west of Char-

Dornier Do 17 Z-2, coded 3Z+BM, of 4./KG 77. Note that the aircraft's individual letter 'B' is repeated under wings in white.

Dornier Do 17 Z of KG 2 'Holzhammer' undergoing a maintenance check.

This Do 17 Z-2, damaged in a shootout with British fighters, was forced to belly-in somewhere in northern France, summer 1940.

leville was the Ardennes. Flying along the Meuse I could safely steer back to base. Heading in that direction we are treated to peaceful, idyllic scenes below, complete with a shepherd boy surrounded by his little herd in the middle of a vast meadow. The war raging a short distance away could not have been more remote from him. At the edge of the Ardennes we again see unmistakable scars left by the war. We pass by a column of enemy vehicles, some of them already on fire. My crew again man the machine guns.

Shortly before reaching the line of the Meuse river I am startled to see a pair of fighters, Curtiss or Morane type, their wings flashing French roundels. They are barely some 100 meters distant. I hit the deck, attempting to

squeeze into a forest glade and sneak away. The dark valley of the Meuse, carved deep into the surrounding landscape, appears to us like a safe haven. We know that our ground troops are nearby. But the danger is not over yet. We cautiously gain some altitude and chance upon a somewhat haphazard formation of machines from our Gruppe. We gladly join in".[23]

On the same day, III./KG 3 was intercepted by French Hawk C.75 fighters of GC II./2 and GC III./7, as well as Hurricanes of No 501 Sqn RAF. The allied fighters shot down three Do 17 Zs. One of the British pilots credited with a victory over a Dornier was Plt/Off Kenneth Lee: "I was ordered to fly rear cover (arse-end Charlie) and I observed bomb bursts below and then spot-

ted four Dornier 17s flying 4,000 feet below. I flew up in front of the section and waggled my wings, pointing down (full radio silence was being maintained so as not to advertise our presence in France). I peeled off towards the enemy and followed the classic procedure: tighten straps, switch on gun button, lower seat, set sight with wingspan of target and range 300 yards. Whilst this was going on, the Dorniers assumed vic, with one in the box. I turned towards them, looking confidently over my shoulder for my supporting friends, assuming they had made formation on me as practiced ad infinitum for a No 2 Fighter Attack – but there was no one there! I was committed and went on alone, with one Dornier down (as confirmed by French artillery) and one damaged – and 37 strikes on my own aircraft".[24]

On 13th and 14th May 1940 the Wehrmacht, actively supported by the Luftwaffe, established bridgeheads on the other side of the Meuse river near Sedan. Again KG 2 distinguished itself, bombing French troops with great precision. Air operations continued at an unabated pace on 15th May. At about 08:00 hrs a group of some 40 Do 17 Zs of I. and III./KG 3, escorted by a dozen twin-engined Messerschmitt Bf 110 Cs of III./ZG 26, was engaged near Reims by Hurricanes of No 1 Sqn RAF. The Messerschmitts beat off the attack, but lost two of their own. While No 1 Sqn kept the escorts busy, the Dorniers were jumped by Hurricanes

Dornier Do 17 Z-2
of Stabsschwarm KG 3, coded
5K+BA, heading for England
in August 1940.

Crew compartment interior of Do 17 Z-2, with Lotfe bombsight visible to the right and at the bottom.

Dornier Do 215 B-4 of 4.(F)/ Aufkl.Gr.Ob.d.L., which was based at Merville and flew reconnaissance missions over British Islands.

of No 501 Sqn RAF. The British shot down one Do 17, but not before two of them fell to the bombers' rear gunners.

Shortly before 11:00 hrs seven Do 17 Zs of 8./KG 76 were challenged by Hurricanes of No 3 Sqn RAF patrolling the Namur area. Again the British pilots' claim of one Do 17 destroyed had to be offset by the loss of two Hurricanes. One was shot down by rear gunners, whilst the other fell prey to Lt. Joachim Müncheberg of III./JG 26, a Bf 109 pilot.

After the breakthrough at Sedan German troops swiftly advanced towards the English Channel. By then the Do 17s were mainly interdicting the retreating columns and hitting concentrations of Allied troops on either side of the German 'corridor' to thwart anticipated counterattacks. On 20th May the German armoured spearheads reached the Channel, cutting off the Belgian army, the British Expeditionary Force and elements of the French army. On 27th May the British began to evacuate by sea through the port of Dunkirk. The Luftwaffe was faced with a difficult task, for the evacuation area lay within the range of RAF fighters stationed in eastern England.

Four flights of Do 17 Zs of III./KG 3, which had bombed a fuel dump west of the harbour, were intercepted by a squadron of Spitfires. The unescorted bombers stood no chance, and in a matter of minutes six of them went down in flames. While this was taking place, Do 17 Zs of II. and III./KG 2 returning to base were bounced by Spitfires of No 65 Sqn RAF, which shot down three Dorniers and seriously damaged three more.

With the allied operation "Dynamo" over, the main Luftwaffe force was directed to support the Wehrmacht advance towards Paris. On 3rd June 1940 the Germans launched operation "Paula" – concentrated attacks against airfields and aviation industry facilities around the French capital. At 13:00 hrs 85 Do 17 Zs of KG 2's three component *Gruppen* struck off for an airfield complex at Villeneuve-Orly. Bombs destroyed hangars and 23 parked aircraft.

The offensive, which was to seal the fate of France, got underway on 5th June 1940.

Again Do 17s hunted down marching columns and concentrations of enemy troops. One such sortie, carried out on 15th June 1940, was recalled by Ofw. Wolff of 6./KG 2 in the following words:

"We attacked the retreating enemy south of Verdun, flying at treetop level. The entire town was in flames. Some strongholds were still under heavy shelling from our artillery. We could see our infantry closing in on them. During the Great War the battle for Verdun had cost the lives of several hundred thousand people. This time that most formidable fortress in France fell after a two-day assault! Our low-level approach paid off, for we detected lots of troops on the ground. After releasing our bombs we strafed the enemy columns.

The French fired back with anti-aircraft cannons and machine guns. We were hit in the tail, and our starboard fuel tank was punctured twice. In addition, a stray bullet went right through the roof of our crew compartment and another whizzed across the fuselage. Both our propellers had bullet holes in them, too".[25]

On 17th June Marshal Pétain sued for an armistice, which came into effect five days later. The Battle for France was over. Operations over western Europe demonstrated that Do 17s were under-armoured and under-armed. Whenever

Dornier Do 17 Z-2s of Geschwaderstab KG 3 passing over London suburbs.

Dornier Do 17 Z-2s of KG 3 returning from a combat mission, August 1940.

faced with staunch opposition in the air, as over Dunkirk, they suffered heavy losses.

Battle of Britain

With the fall of France, the only adversary of the Third Reich was the British Empire. Hitler hoped for peace negotiations, but the British government headed by Winston Churchill flatly rejected his offer. Initially, the Luftwaffe limited its scope of operations to harassing coastal convoys. The first such mission was flown on 4th July 1940, when 18 Do 17 Zs of II./KG 2, escorted by 30 Bf 109 Es of JG 51, attacked a convoy of nine ships headed for Dover. One of the ships was hit and later beached in coastal shallows. No 79 Sqn RAF, which was scrambled to chase off the intruders, lost one Hurricane in the ensuing melee. Three days later 45 Do 17 Zs of

II. and III./KG 2, escorted by Bf 109 Es of JG 27, targeted another convoy bound for Dover. This time the Germans sank one ship and damaged three more. Intervening Spitfires of No 46 Sqn RAF damaged two Dorniers, which crash-landed in France.

10th July 1940 witnessed the first air battle worthy of the name over the Channel. On that day a coastal convoy came under attack from 26 Do 17 Zs of I. and III./KG 2. One ship was sunk. No fewer than 100 aircraft clashed over the convoy. The Germans lost one Dornier (flown by Hptm. Krieger, the *Staffelkapitän* of 3./KG 2), which was rammed by a Hurricane (F/O Higgs) of No 111 Sqn RAF.

During that period reconnaissance Do 17 Ps were equally active over the Channel, spying on convoys and reporting back their position.

Dornier Do 17 Z-2 sporting the emblem of its parent Gruppe, I./KG 77.

However, venturing singly into enemy airspace was always a hazardous business. On 13th July 1940 a Do 17 P of 2.(F)/123 (flown by Lt. Weinbauer) failed to return to base. Another Dornier, a Do 17 M of 4.(F)/14, got away with only slight damage (10%). Six days later Hurricanes of 257 and 145 Sqns RAF shot down a Do 17 P of 1.(F)/121 (flown by Lt. Thiele).

On 13th August 1940 came the *Adlertag* (Eagle's Day), which heralded the beginning of the Luftwaffe offensive against the British Isles. Morning mists delayed the launch of the attack until the afternoon. However, 74 Do 17 Zs of KG 2, which were already up in the air by the time the mission was scrapped, missed the order to turn back. When the high command realized that the *Geschwaderkommodore* Obst. Johannes Fink had not acknowledged the order (his radio was broken), four Bf 110s were scrambled to visually signal to Obst. Fink that he should return. The *Zerstörer* pilots performed every imaginable aerobatic manoeuvre in front of the Dorniers in order to attract their attention. However, Obst. Fink came to the conclusion that he was being

Dornier Do 17 Z-1, coded U5＋GH, of 1./KG 2 'Holzhammer' at Epinoy airfield, France, September 1940.

Dornier Do 17 Z-2s of KG 3 crossing the English Channel.

Bombs away over a target in southeast England.

treated to a spontaneous demonstration of eagerness for combat, and pressed on. His target was Eastchurch airbase. British spotters wrongly estimated the approaching force at only a dozen or so machines, hence only a single RAF fighter squadron was scrambled to intercept. Only after the airfield had been bombed, did two more British fighter squadrons join in the scrap. The German raid destroyed five Blenheims on the ground, a command post and severely cratered the landing field; 12 men were killed and 40 injured. During the skirmish in the air the bombers' gunners claimed one Spitfire, but the German losses amounted to five aircraft destroyed and seven damaged.

On Thursday 15th August 1940 as many as 88 Do 17 Zs of KG 3, escorted by nearly 130 Bf 109 Es, ventured over England. Despite ferocious attacks by the RAF, they could claim only two Dorniers, for the loss of five fighters. Over Faversham the Dornier formation split up – the *Stabskette*, I. and II./KG 3 turned towards Rochester, whilst III./KG 3 went after Eastchurch airfield. In Rochester, over 300 bombs hit the Short Bros aviation plant and airfield. They destroyed the company's assembly hall and magazines, where components of Stirling heavy bombers were stored. As a result of that

raid production at the plant was interrupted for three months.

The following day, 16th August 1940, the Do 17s were equally successful. Two *Staffeln* of KG 2 sneaked undetected over West Malling airfield, where they unloaded over 80 bombs. Besides a solitary Lysander destroyed on the ground, damage to the airfield facilities was so serious that it was effectively knocked out of action for four days. The Germans lost three bombers.

On 26th August 1940, at about 13:00 hrs, West Malling was again bombed, this time by Do 17s of III./KG 3. The raiders paid a high price – four Dorniers were shot down and one damaged. Two hours later over 40 Do 17 Zs of KG 2 targeted airfields at Debden and Hornchurch. Again the German losses were disproportionate to their successes, for the British interceptors shot down six Do 17s, including the machines flown by the *Gruppenkommandeur* of I./KG 2 Maj. Martin Gutzmann and the *Staffelkapitän* of 3./KG 2, Oblt. Hermann Buchholz.

On the last day of August 1940 a formation of Do 17s of II. and III./KG 2, setting out to strike Duxford aerodrome, was intercepted over Colchester by Hurricanes of No 111 Sqn RAF. The attack was so furious and persistent that the

Battle-damaged Dornier Do 17 Zs often crashed on landing.

oppressed Dornier crews jettisoned their bombloads and hightailed for France. Among the injured was the *Gruppenkommandeur* of III./KG 2 Maj. Adolf Fuchs. KG 3 fared no better. At about 13:30 hrs I. and II. *Gruppen* bombed Hornchurch station, but lost four bombers (with five more damaged) to intervening RAF fighters. On 7th September 1940 the Luftwaffe commenced daylight bomb raids on London. At 16:45 hrs 27 crews of II./KG 2 and 24 of III./KG 2 got airborne for their first attack against Victoria and India Docks on the Thames river. In the ensuing scrap with British fighters one Do 17 Z of 4./KG 2 was shot down.

The apogee of the Battle of Britain came on 15th September 1940. The first wave of the attack consisted of 27 Do 17 Zs of KG 76 shepherded by nearly 180 Bf 109 Es. The defenders scrambled ten fighter squadrons to contest this incursion. Six Dorniers failed to return, and two more were damaged. Some two hours later the second wave of bombers, comprising Do 17 Zs of KG 2 and KG 3 under Obstlt. Von Chamier-Glisczynski, arrived over London. Horst Zander, a radio operator of 6./KG 3, was onboard one of the Dorniers:

"I'm scanning the sky all around us. To the left and right of us I can see machines of our Staffel comrades, further away the rest of II. Gruppe. Behind and ahead of us, slightly above, are the remaining Gruppen of our Geschwader.

A British soldier with a 7.92 mm MG 15 machine gun extracted from a wreck of a Do 17 Z-2; England, autumn 1940.

The emblem of IV.(Erg.)/KG 3 painted under the cockpit of a Dornier Do 17 Z-2; France winter of 1940/41.

High above there's our escort. 'Only the English are missing…' I thought.

As we reach Canterbury, KG 3 encounters the first enemy fighters. In my headset I can hear the voice of our observer and the commander of our crew, Oblt. Laube, who calmly calls out: 'Fighters ahead!'

The air fills with the hollow thud of numerous machine guns firing. Two gun bursts whizz past our machine. Two British fighters collided with two bombers from our Gruppe. Their burning wrecks plunge down. A few parachute canopies pop open below. We look at one another and give a thumbs-up. We got away unscathed from this mess.

We have to tighten our formation and fill in the gaps. We continue towards London. After a dozen or so minutes we are over the target. Bombs away, and we gladly bid our farewell to England. But at that same instant enemy fighters reappear. The defensive formation of our Gruppe is shattered. From now on each crew must fight separately for their own survival. Most dive for the deck, and at full bore, skimming the waves of the Channel, make a run for France.

All of a sudden our machine shudders under a hefty blow. Flames spring up, and black smoke fills the cockpit. Icy air streams inside the crew compartment through the shattered windscreen. The entire cockpit is spattered with blood. Our pilot was hit. In my earphones I can hear his faint voice, 'Heinz, get us home!'

In the meantime we fly out to the North Sea, and the pilot and observer can switch seats. Our flight engineer immediately attends to the pilot's injuries. Oblt. Laube, our observer and commander, flies the machine like an old hand. Although his pilot licence covers only light sports aircraft, twenty minutes after taking over the controls he lands our shot-up crate, albeit with a few bumps, at an airfield in Antwerp".[26]

The losses suffered by the two Do 17 *Kampfgeschwadern* were unacceptably high – eight machines in KG 2, and six in KG 3.

A reconnaissance Dornier Do 215 B-4 crashed as a result of a forced landing.

MONOGRAFIE MONOGRAPHS

Operations over England proved beyond any doubt that the Do 17 Z was woefully vulnerable to intercepting fighters. It was poorly armoured, inadequately armed and too slow to outrun its pursuers.

Campaign in the Balkans – spring 1941

Due to unexpected turmoil in the Balkans triggered by the Italians, their German allies, alarmed by the arrival of British troops in Greece, resolved to neutralise what they perceived as a threat to their southern flank. Among the Luftwaffe units selected for opera-

tion "Marita" were several Do 17 *Geschwadern* (see the appendix).

At 06:45 hrs Do 17 Zs of KG 2 and KG 3 turned up over Belgrade. They were challenged by nearly the entire 6th Fighter Regiment of the Royal Yugoslav Air Force, a unit equipped with, among other types, Messerschmitt Bf 109 Es. Lt. Heinrich Meyer of 2./KG 2 recalled:

"There, what was that? Streaks of tracers flash by, right between our machine and the machines of my two wingmen. Enemy fighters! I put my steel helmet on and grab my machine gun. This smart fellow must have sneaked up on us from behind. I can't see him yet. Now my

Dornier Do 17 Z-3 armed with eight 7.92 mm MG 15 machine guns on flexible mounts, photographed in France at the turn of 1940/41.

Dornier Do 17 Z-2 of I./KG 2 at Plovdiv airfield in central Bulgaria, April 1941. Noteworthy are quick air-to-air recognition markings in form of yellow engine cowlings and rudders. Note open ventral entry hatch. (This photo and from next page)

A crew of I./KG 2's Dornier Do 17 Z-2 awaiting another combat sortie at Plovdiv, Bulgaria, in April 1941.

flight engineer opens up. 'Enemy Me 109!' he yells at the top of his voice.

The enemy fighter half-rolls to port and split-esses away from us, manoeuvring for another firing pass. The machine on the right flank of our flight immediately drops lower to offer the remaining aircraft a better field of fire. The enemy pilot is very cautious. He closes down to 100 meters, and then breaks off his attack, zooming up. We can only take a few pot shots at his belly. He again bores in from the same direction but he's still too far away. However,

during another pass he finally cuts the distance down to 50 meters, and when he breaks off, his entire undersides are there for us to aim at. That was his undoing. A long burst tears into his belly. He hurtles straight down, spouting a trail of white smoke, and he's gone for good. Another victory for my flight, and the fifth for 2. Staffel. Both my wingmen return to base each with some 20 bullet holes in their machines".[27]

Among the German losses after this raid were two Do 17 Zs of KG 3. In the ensuing days Do 17s participated in attacks on Belgrade,

Dornier Do 17 Z-2 of KG 2 during the campaign in Greece.

A flight of Dornier Do 17 Z-2s of KG 2 passing over the Athens.

Dornier Do 17 Z-1, coded 3U+FU, of 10./ZG 26 'Horst Wessel', captured by the British in the Western Desert; Libya, December 1941.

bombed Yugoslav army columns, railway lines and marshalling yards.

Concurrently with the invasion of Yugoslavia the Germans mounted an operation against Greece and the British Expeditionary Force supporting the Greeks. Since the Luftwaffe had quickly won air superiority, most interdiction missions were carried out by freelancing flights of unescorted bombers, which searched and destroyed columns of enemy troops. An intense air battle, which cost KG 2 four aircraft, took place in the Piraeus area on 20th April.

Two days later the *Geschwader* set upon Argos airfield in the Peloponnesus peninsula, destroying five British fighters and one Greek trainer on the ground. Overall, during operations over the Balkans in April 1941 the Luftwaffe lost 29 Do 17 Ps and Zs.

In a report prepared by VIII. Fliegerkorps, which summarized the tactical experience gained over Yugoslavia and Greece, some remarks referred to Do 17s' operations:

"4. Attacks on marching troop columns were effective only when performed at low alti-

Dornier Do 17 Z's rudder sporting a victory marking – one Allied ship sunk. Mediterranean Theatre of Operations, spring 1942.

tude. However, since enemy vehicles were usually well spaced out, losses to ground fire were high. Hence, it is advisable to carry out such attacks with the advantage of surprise, making clever use of terrain configuration, lighting, position of the sun, etc. Points of resistance, which were encountered in numbers along the enemy's route of withdrawal, ought to be neutralized from medium altitudes (…)

5. Troop concentrations located near bridges, mountain passes, around barracks and the like were effectively engaged from medium altitudes, with no losses. A well-camouflaged enemy was not easily recognizable from the air – hence many crews refrained from bombing copses of trees, forests or plantations, even though aerial reconnaissance had earlier confirmed an enemy presence there. Notwithstanding the fact that from an altitude of 300-500 metres identifying enemy troops on the ground was often impossible, such suspected areas are nevertheless to be bombed without hesitation. The best weapons against such targets are SD 2 bombs, which unfortunately were unavailable at the time.

6. Operations against shipping confirmed that the Do 17 Z was ill-suited for this type of mission; 50 kg bombs dropped from medium altitude proved ineffective against ships over 1,000 GRT. Using adequate munitions (250 kg bombs with armour-piercing warheads) was not possible due to shortages of supplies".[28]

Operation "Marita" was directly followed by preparations to the invasion of Crete. Operation "Merkur", as it was code-named, was launched at dawn of 20th May 1941. Between 07:00 and 07:15 hrs 59 Do 17 Zs of KG 2 bombed British positions around airfields in

Dornier Do 17 Z-2 of KG 3 photographed during the first winter on the eastern front.

Dornier Do 17 Z-2, coded 5K+MR, of 7./KG 3; Russia, December 1941.

Maleme and Chania. The Dorniers encountered withering anti-aircraft fire. A Do 17 (W.Nr. 2777, coded U5+EH) flown by Oblt. Schmidt was hit in one engine, which after a while quit working. The machine turned back for Greece. Despite desperate efforts by the crew – who tossed equipment overboard to lighten the limping machine – it kept losing height until it ditched some 40 kilometres from Kythira island. The Dornier instantly sank. Only the pilot, Oblt. Schmidt and a gunner, Ofw. Fall, managed to extricate themselves from the doomed aircraft. However, the jagged edges of some damaged metal panels ripped the gunner's life vest, and he drowned before he could be rescued. Oblt. Schmidt was picked up from the sea several hours later by an Italian patrol boat.

On the first day of operations over Crete some crews flew as many as three sorties. In the evening KG 2 suffered another loss, when an anti-aircraft shell set fire to one of the engines in Do 17 Z W.Nr. 3418, coded U5+BH. Its pilot, Lt. Max Graf von Dürkheim, attempted to belly-land some four kilometres southwest of Chania, but the aircraft crashed in the rugged terrain of the island and burst into flames. Its entire crew perished. The following day engine failure, caused by a malfunction or battle damage, forced Maj. Heinrich Eichhorn, the *Gruppenkom-*

mandeur of III./KG 2, to crash-land on Crete. He was captured with his crew.

Throughout 22nd May 1941 Do 17 Zs of KG 2 and KG 3 concentrated their attacks against Royal Navy ships. On that day the Luftwaffe sank two cruisers, "Gloucester" and "Fiji", and the destroyer "Greyhound". Moreover, bombs damaged the battleships "Warspite" and "Valiant", as well as the cruisers "Naiad" and "Carlisle". Nevertheless, the most telling damage was inflicted by Stukas and fighter-bomber Bf 109 Es armed with 250 kg bombs.

In the early hours of 23rd May 1941 Dorniers bombed and damaged two Royal Navy destroyers, "Kashmir" and "Kelly", which were shortly afterwards finished off by Ju 87s of St.G 2. The last success scored by KG 2 against the Royal Navy on the waters around Crete came on 28th May 1941, when Do 17 Zs hit the destroyer "Imperial". The severely damaged ship was finished off the following day by another British destroyer, the "Hotspur".

Overall, during the campaign in the Balkans KG 2 lost a total of 12 aircraft to enemy action and another six to other causes. Moreover, 26 machines were damaged, including 13 with over 50% damage. Of flying personnel losses, 37 airmen were killed, 15 posted missing, and 35 injured.

Operation "Barbarossa"

On the eve of the war with the Soviet Union, most of the 29 *Kampfgruppen* earmarked for operation "Barbarossa" were equipped with either Heinkel He 111s or Junkers Ju 88s. Only three *Gruppen* still operated Dornier Do 17 Zs.

At about 02:15 hrs, on 22nd June 1941, the first Do 17s of KG 2, manned only by the crews most experienced and trained in 'blind flying', took to the air in predawn darkness. Their targets were airfields in the immediate vicinity of the border. Crews of 9./KG 2 were briefed to cut a strategic railway line, which ran from the east to Vilnius.

At the break of day more Dorniers of KG 2 followed. Among them was Do 17 Z, W.Nr. 3603, coded U5+DA, assigned to *Stabsstaffel/ KG 2*, and crewed by Ofw. Erich Stockmann (pilot), Oblt. Hans-Georg Peters (observer), Fw. Hans Kownatzki (radio operator), and Uffz. Hans Schuhmacher (gunner). Fw. Kornatzki related the events of this dramatic mission in the following words:

"On 22nd June we took off on a mission to strike at a Soviet airfield. At 04:45 hrs, 24 kilometres southeast of Łomża, near Zambrów, we were jumped by enemy fighters. We managed to knock down three of the assailants. In the shootout with fighters two bullets grazed my head. Moments later we were shot down. Our machine spun down. Oberleutnant Peters and I were thrown clear of the cockpit by centrifugal forces and landed on our parachutes in a grainfield. A Polish civilian found us. He told us that our two comrades, Ofw. Stockmann and Uffz. Schuhmacher, went down with the machine and were killed. When the aircraft went into a spin, I was thrown about the cockpit and badly battered. Oberleutnant Peters had a broken left leg. I immobilized it with two branches. The Pole who found us brought us something to eat and drink, and cared after us for the following two hours. After we had remained hidden all day in that cornfield, Oblt. Peters ordered me to try to break through by myself, to rejoin friendly lines across the Narew river. His fractured leg wouldn't allow him to accompany me. He also suffered from intense pain in his back, and due to an injury to his left eyelid his field of vision was limited. Hence, I set out on my own. In a nearby forest clearing I came across some retreating Soviet troops and again had to seek cover. I spent a night at a Polish peasant's house. There, at about 05:00 hrs, most unexpectedly Oblt. Peters turned up. We decided to continue together and immediately moved on.

On our way we often had to hide from Soviet troops marching en masse in the opposite direction. We took cover in a large grainfield. However, at about eight or nine in the morning, the Russians began to thoroughly search the area, and soon we were discovered. Perhaps some Poles who had pastured a herd of cattle nearby tipped them off. As soon as we were spotted by one of the soldiers, he fired his rifle in the air to alert his comrades, and they all came running towards us. We were ordered to stand up and raise our hands. They tore off our uniforms, leaving us in our underwear. They seemed very content to have captured a German officer. We were beaten and clubbed with rifle butts. All that time we had to keep our hands up. Our arms quickly went numb, but

Dornier Do 17 Z-2 of 15.(kroat.)/KG 3. Note the unit's emblem under cockpit.

Dornier Do 17 Z-7 'Kauz I' of 2./NJG 2 painted overall black, spring 1941.

Dornier Do 17 P-1 of 1.(F)/Aufkl.Gr. Nacht, a night reconnaissance group, which in late 1942 operated in the eastern front.

when we dared to lower them, we were again punched.

At first there were no Russian officers to be seen around. Oblt. Peters, as soon as we were captured, demanded to see an officer, but he was simply laughed at. Finally, four or five officers came up. They had one or two stars pinned to their collars, and wore two or three big chevrons on their left sleeves. Some of the Russians could speak a broken German. They called us 'SOBs' and 'Nazi pigs', and accused us of murdering innocent people. For the next two hours we were marched with hands up, barefoot and

in our underwear only, along a muddy, dirt road. I walked ahead, with Oblt. Peters behind me. We couldn't help lowering our tired arms, which only spurred our captors to beat us some more with rifle butts. A Russian officer, who looked no more than 20 or 21 years old, lashed Oblt. Peters numerous times with a whip.

After about two hours suddenly we stopped. Some five to six kilometres to the north there was a major road, which ran parallel to ours. We could see billowing dust over there. The Russians instantly left the road we had used and began to set up their artillery pieces in an

adjacent cornfield. They attempted to pry some information of military value from us, names of locations where our units were stationed, details of our equipment and the like. After about a half an hour we resumed our march. Initially we walked back some distance, then turned north. Finally we reached the main highway. I suspected it was the Ostrów – Białystok road. We kept marching, barefoot and with our hands up, until 19:00 hrs. In the meantime we were neither fed nor given anything to drink. As we were passing through Polish villages, their occupants offered us water, but the Russians chased them away. Only once did a Russian soldier bring us a helmet full of black, miry water from a nearby pond, but we were so thirsty that we drank it all. During one of the stops, which lasted for about half an hour, a Russian officer, who could speak German, approached us. He was most probably a medical officer, since the soldiers addressed him as Doctor. He wanted to take care of Oblt. Peters, whose eyelid was still bleeding, but was immediately scolded by a higher-ranking officer. At about 20:00 hrs we arrived at the village of Zambrzyce Stare. There, we again were brought in front of higher-ranking officers, who interrogated us. When we refused to talk, we were led to a fenced potato field next to the Ostrów – Białystok road. We leaned our backs against the wall of a shed, which stood in the corner of the field. Mounted guards armed with rifles were positioned on either end of the field. The only relief was that the Polish civilians were allowed to bring us water. We asked to be given back our trousers,

because it was getting cold, but our pleas were turned down.

At about 21:00 hrs we caught the sound of rifle fire, and an artillery shell, most probably a large calibre mortar round, exploded nearby. Oblt. Peters exclaimed; 'Kownatzki, Germans are coming!' We jumped among the potato beds. I hugged the ground, trying to avoid being hit by shrapnel. At the same instant I noticed that one of the two horse-mounted guards had fled, but the other pointed his rifle at us and repeatedly fired. The first bullet got me in my thigh and crushed the bone, then another bullet went through my right arm. I yelled, 'Herr Oberleutnant, I was hit!' He didn't respond. As it transpired, he had received a fatal shot in his back. Moments later the other guard also ran away. Then at night, at about 01:00 hrs, two Russian officers showed up at the potato field. I spotted them in the glow of the moon. They stopped by me, then by Oblt. Peters. I froze motionless and held my breath. The two Russians took us for dead and walked away. I lay between tomato beds until, at about 05:00 hrs, the owner of the field came up and took me to the shed. The Pole took good care of me, washed me, dressed my wounds and fed me. Then he saw to it that a German patrol passing by picked me up".[29]

The Dornier was attacked by MiG-3 and I-16 fighters of 124 IAP / 9 SAD led by Mladshiy Leytenant Dmitriy Kokorev. The Russians lost three fighters to return fire. Kokorev, after he had expended all his ammunition, performed the first ramming attack. He crashed the propeller of his MiG-3 into a German bomber's empen-

Dornier Do 17 Ps of the Bulgarian Air Force.

nage, whereupon he managed to regain control over his fighter and belly-land near Zambrów. For this deed he was later awarded the Order of the Red Banner. Kokorev went on to fly 100 more combat sorties before he was killed in aerial combat in October 1941.

During the ensuing two days Do 17s of KG 2 were engaged in bombing Soviet armoured units around the city of Grodno. Hptm. Walter Brandel, the *Staffelkapitän* of 9./KG 2, which distinguished itself most during those battles, was awarded the Knight's Cross. Actions against Russian airbases proved equally devastating. On 5th July 1941 III./KG 2 and III./KG 3 raided an aerodrome at Vitebsk, where they destroyed 22 aircraft besides some hangars and other airfield facilities.

On the night of 21st/22nd July 1941 Do 17 Zs of I./KG 2, 9./KG 2 and III./KG 3 participated in the first Luftwaffe bombing raid against Moscow. Ofw. Broich of 3./KG 2 reminisced:

"Our order reads – night strike at Moscow, altitude 3,000 metres. We teamed up with III./KG 3. Our machines carried the standard daylight camouflage; they were not repainted black for night operations. We didn't know what to think of it all.

The flight toward the target dragged on. Perhaps it felt that way because we were flying east, towards the dawning day. The sky on the horizon began to grow lighter. On our way we witnessed numerous fires, raging far below, and occasional muzzle flashes of artillery. We tried to stay calm, but were anxious anyway, for this action was very much different from our previous missions.

From a distance we could see that the raid was already on. Finally we arrived at the target and dropped our bombload at the assigned spot.

A Do 17P in Bulgarian Air Force markings.

Suddenly a searchlight lit us up. Instantly, more of them zeroed in on us. A clutch of some 30 beams held us in their cone of light. Anti-aircraft shells began to burst all around. We jettisoned our remaining bombs and began to dodge the Flak.[30] Our pilot, Uffz. Heimann, was constantly changing our altitude and engine revolutions to throw off the Russian gunners' aim and slip away. Our flight engineer Hans tossed overboard bundles of propaganda leaflets, like we had done over England, but it didn't help much. Peter chose to dive towards the part of the city that seemed least defended. We picked up some speed in our dive and got away in one piece. From then on we continued unmolested towards Vitebsk".[31]

Not all the crews were so lucky that night. Near the border the Do 17 Z coded 5K+ET of 9./KG 3, flown by Lt. Kurt Kuhn, was shot down by a famous test pilot Kapitan Mark Gallay.

Hitler's Directive No 34, issued on 30th July 1941, changed the focal point of the German offensive from the central sector of the front to the north. His troops were now to concentrate on cutting off Leningrad and establish contact with the Finns. Luftflotte 1, which was scheduled to support this operation, was strengthened by VIII. Fliegerkorps and its Do 17 Zs of I. and III./KG 2 as well as III./KG 3. The air operations were markedly intense. On 14th August 1941 alone, KG 2 carried out 155 sorties. Losses were inevitable. The machine flown by Lt. Heinrich Hunger, a Knight's Cross holder, was hit by Flak in the port wing right by the engine, which burst into flames. The crew bailed out. After Novgorod had been captured, advancing German troops found the mangled bodies of Lt. Hunger and his radio operator Uffz. Grützner,

murdered by the Soviets. The remaining crew-members were posted missing.

Three days later the commander of VIII. Fliegerkorps *General der Flieger* Wolfram von Richthofen complimented the commander of the *Stabsstaffel*/KG 2 in a congratulatory letter, which described in detail the daring actions of the unit:

"Whilst returning from a combat sortie, Oberleutnant Lutter, the CO of Stabsstaffel/KG 2, spotted a German column threatened by an approaching group of some 30 Russian tanks. Upon landing at his base he immediately refuelled and rearmed, whereupon he scrambled back into the air, accompanied by another flight. The aircraft he led attacked the enemy tanks one by one, flying at a mere 50-100 metres.

Meanwhile, another flight of the Stabsstaffel joined in. All in all, they knocked out 18 tanks in this single action. The remaining tanks fell back in panic. During the attack one of the bomb aimers was killed by ground fire. Oblt. Lutter's bold action scattered a concentration of enemy armour, saved the German column from annihilation, and considerably relieved our troops in this sector of the front. I wish to thank Oblt. Lutter and the crews under his command for such unfailing devotion to their duty."[32]

Bulgarian Do 17Ps taxiing to the runway.

Bomb loading onto a "Bulgarian" Do 17.

In the first part of September 1941 the Do 17s of KG 2 concentrated their efforts on Leningrad. On 15th September 1941 the KG 2 HQ issued a resume of successes scored by the *Geschwader* thus far during operation "Barbarossa":

– 12 enemy aircraft destroyed in the air
– 338 aircraft destroyed on the ground
– 192 tanks destroyed
– 194 artillery pieces destroyed
– 2,427 vehicles destroyed
– 21 fuel dumps, supply and ammunition depots destroyed
– 390 damaged or partially destroyed freight trains
– 134 railway cuts
– 5 bridges destroyed
– 358 points of resistance bombed.[33]

In the period between 17th and 27th September 1941 Dornier Do 17 Zs operated mainly against enemy columns and troop concentrations in the area of Lake Ladoga. In late September 1941, prior to the planned thrust against Moscow, KG 2 was relocated to Vitebsk. Uffz. Gelzenleichter of 3./KG 2 recounted a sortie flown on 10th October 1941:

"We took off (our crew's commander was Uffz. Stumpf) in our Do 17 for an armed reconnaissance mission behind enemy lines. Our task was to seek and destroy enemy positions, supply lines and the like.

Shortly after take-off we waded into thick clouds. The cloud deck was at some 900 meters. We crossed the lines unnoticed, hidden in the overcast. At 1,200 meters we broke into clear blue sky. Visibility was excellent. This meant we had to be on the lookout for enemy fighters. In the distance we noticed several Stukas, which were tackling some target of their own, but the enemy Ratas[34] were nowhere to be seen.

Suddenly the curtain of clouds below us drew aside. Lying in the ventral gondola, I saw a big railway station with three freight trains. I immediately alerted our 'coachman'[35], who dropped the port wing to have a closer look.

Since no enemy fighters had turned up so far and no one had fired at us from the ground, we decided to attack the station. We flew over it, parallel to the tracks. The cloudbank overhead offered sufficient protection, should things get too hot for us. Bomb bay doors flipped open, and our bomb aimer lined up the target in his sights. The first bombs dropped away and we ducked into the clouds.

Suddenly, a powerful force gripped our aircraft. The nose pitched sharply up, and then the aircraft hurtled down. I was yanked towards the cockpit roof, but at the last instant I managed to grab the machine gun butt and prevent my fall. Initially we didn't know what had happened. Uffz. Stumpf got the machine under control. As we were leaving the area, through a break in

Do 17 Z-10 (coded CD + PV) was used as a flying testbed to help develop the FuG 202 'Lichtenstein C-1' airborne radar set.

the clouds I saw that we had hit an ammunition train!"[36]

With the arrival of autumn downpours in the latter part of October 1941, the German offensive literally got stuck in a sea of mire. At the same time the component *Staffeln* of KG 2 and III./KG 3 were successively rotated to Germany to convert onto modern Dornier Do 217s.

Besides the Luftwaffe, reconnaissance and bomber outfits of the Axis cobelligerent forces also operated Do 17s. In the years 1940-41 Bulgaria received 11 Dorniers of the Kb1 version and 12 Do 17 Ps, followed by 12 Do 17 Ms in 1943. In early 1942 Finland got 15 Do 17 Zs, which flew their first combat mission on 1st April 1942. One Do 17 was operated by the ROA (Russian Liberation Army). The Croatian Air Force was issued with 11 Do 17 Ks and 36 Do 17 Es between 1942 and 1943. The Croats also operated on the eastern front on Do 17 Zs with 15.(kroat.)/KG 3 and 15.(kroat.)/KG 53. The Hungarian Air Force is known to have operated eight Do 215 B-4s.

Dornier Do 17 Z-7 and Z-10 night fighters

Do 17 Z-7s "Kauz I" and Z-10s "Kauz II" on strength with 2./NJG 2 took an active part in combating the RAF night bombers. They carried out *Fernnachtjagd* missions (night intruder operations) over England, stalking returning British bombers in the vicinity of their bases. Debriefing reports by the crews that flew the missions tell their stories:

Combat report

Crew: Hptm. Jung, Uffz. Schurks, Uffz. Thomas

Date: 11th/12th February 1941

Aircraft flown: Do 17

Take-off at 23:45 hrs, landing at 03:46 hrs, time spent in operation area: between 01:00 and 03:00 hrs

"Four aircraft were observed in a landing circuit at airfield 10280 (lights on the ground were on). Our aircraft was detected too early and the runway lights switched off. Between 01:00 and 01:45 hrs we made three passes, dropping a total of 120 incendiary bombs on hangars and billets. The attacks were carried out from an altitude of 500 metres. Numerous and sustained fires were noted. During six subsequent low-level runs firefighter units were strafed. At 02:20 hrs six machines circling over airfield 10242 were spotted. During an attack on one of them, carried out at an altitude of 100 metres, the targeted bomber switched off its position lights and the subsequent chase proved ineffective. At 02:30 hrs one Wellington bomber was shot down near airfield 10242, at an altitude of 200 metres. After firing two bursts its starboard engine caught fire, then the aircraft blew up in mid-

air. Light anti-aircraft batteries opened up, hitting our machine six times. At 03:00 hrs, in the vicinity of Great Yarmouth, at an altitude of 800 metres, we fired three bursts at a Bristol Blenheim. The bomber had previously fired red and yellow signal flares. We clearly saw our bursts find their mark and the flames they caused. Further observation of the bomber was not possible. Its ultimate destruction was highly probable."

Combat Report

Crew: Oblt. Schulz, Uffz. Krüger, Ogfr. Lüttringhaus

Take-off at 23:50 hrs, Landing at 03:51 hrs, time spent in operational area: 01:00 – 03:00 hrs

Aircraft flown: Do 17

"Destruction of a Bristol Blenheim at 01:00 hrs near airfield 10242. The engagement took place at 200 metres altitude, from a distance of 100 metres. After our first burst the attacked bomber's port engine broke off its mounting. The actual crash was not observed since British night fighters, of Defiant or Spitfire type, attacked our aircraft. We were fired upon four times, but ineffectively. At 02:05 hrs we dropped 120 incendiary bombs from 800 metres on airfield 10841. Numerous, sustained fires were ignited in barracks and airfield facilities. Special note: British anti-aircraft artillery kept firing despite the presence of their bombers overhead. No searchlights were observed. In the northern part of the C area two to three night fighters were active. British night fighters were also spotted circling among landing aircraft at the target 10242".

Combat report

Crew: Lt. Feuerbaum, Gefr. Denzin, Uffz. Funke.

Take-off at 00:07 hrs, landing at 04:01 hrs, time spent in the operational area: 01:00 – 03:00 hrs

Aircraft flown: Do 17

"At 02:10 hrs, near airfield 10144 and at 300 metres, we engaged a Wellington bomber in a landing pattern. We observed numerous hits and two fires, in the fuselage and port wing. As we passed over the bomber, our rear gunner shot at it. Further hits were scored in the bomber's fuselage mid-section. Although not witnessed, the destruction of the aircraft was very probable. Immediately after this engagement we dropped 120 incendiary bombs from an altitude of 300 metres over target no 10144. Sustained fires were observed".[37]

Hitler's order, issued in October 1941, put an end to operations by German night intruders over England. Shortly afterwards the worn-out Do 17 and Do 215 night fighters were withdrawn from active service.

Endnotes

1. Actually PZL P.11s (author's note).
2. Oblt. Pritzel's account quoted after *Unsere Flieger über Polen*, General der Flieger Kesselring (Ed.), Berlin 1939, pp. 13-19.
3. DLH – *Deutsche Lufthansa*, German national air line.
4. Based on "The Annals of the 'Pencil', the story of the first-generation Dornier Do 17", Air Enthusiast/Thirty, pp. 38-53.
5. Protocol Do 17 V1/256/743 dated to 19th July1935.
6. Based on "The Annals of the 'Pencil' p. 42.
7. Based on „The Annals of the 'Pencil'..., p. 43.
8. Some sources claim that each of the three aircraft was powered by a different variant of the DB 601 engine: the S-1 by the DB 601 A, the S-2 by the DB 601 B, and the S-3 by the DB 601 N, which doesn't seem very likely.
9. Zugspitze – highest mountain in Germany (2964 m), located at the Austrian border in the district of Garmisch-Partenkirchen, Bavaria (author's note).
10. The Nuremberg Rally (officially *Reichsparteitag*) was the annual rally of the NSDAP (Nazi Party) in the years 1923 to 1938 in Germany (translator's note).
11. Aufdemkamp Friedrich: *Wir flogen mit dem Edelweiß*, Waizendorf 2002, pp. 70-71.
12. The two aircraft coded 27•1 and 27•2 were E-1 models, whilst the other two were F-1s.
13. Felipe del Rio Crespo, a seven-victory ace, was killed in action only four days later, on 22nd April 1937. He fell victim to Lt. Radusch of 2.J/88, a Bf 109 B pilot.
14. Ries Karl, Ring Hans: *The Legion Condor*, West Chester 1992, p. 62.
15. The bombing of Guernica, immortalized by Pablo Picasso in his famous painting under the same title, came to symbolize the terror of modern air warfare.
16. The aircraft coded 7 and 8 were F-1 models.
17. Cynk Jerzy B., *Polskie lotnictwo myśliwskie w boju wrześniowym*, Gdańsk 2000.
18. Literally a 'chained dog', in the Luftwaffe vernacular one of two wingmen in a flight of three (author's note).
19. Quoted after: Emmerling Marius: *Luftwaffe nad Polską 1939*, cz. II Kampfflieger, Grynia 2005, p. 34.
20. Data after: Emmerling, p. 304.
21. For the list of the Luftwaffe units equipped with the Do 17, see appendix 2.
22. Balke Ulf: *Der Luftkrieg in Europa, Die operativen Einsätze des Kampfgeschwaders 2 im Zweiten Weltkrieg, Teil 1: Das Luftkriegsgeschehen 1939-1941*, Koblenz 1989, pp. 74-76.
23. Ibidem, op. cit. pp. 85-86.
24. Quoted after: Cull Brian, Lander Bruce, Weiss Heinrich: *Twelve days in May*, London 1995, p. 88.
25. Balke..., op. cit. p. 123.
26. Murawski Marek J.: *Luftwaffe – działania bojowe*, Warszawa 1998, p. 155.
27. Balke..., op. cit. p. 237.
28. Balke, op. cit., p. 273.
29. Balke, op. cit., pp. 308-310.
30. Fliegerabwehrkanone – (Ger.) anti-aircraft gun, a common expression denoting anti-aircraft artillery during the Second world War (author's note).
31. Regnat Karl-Heinz: *Vom Original zum Model: Dornier Do 17*, Bonn 2005, pp. 82-83.
32. Balke, op. cit., p. 348.
33. Ibidem, op. cit. p. 365.
34. Rata – in the Luftwaffe's vernacular a popular nickname of Russian Polikarpov I-16 fighter (author's note).
35. Kutscher – a coachman, in the Luftwaffe's vernacular a bomber pilot (author's note).
36. Balke, op. cit. pp. 377-378.
37. Regnat, op. cit., pp. 86-87.

Dornier Do 17 M-1 (coded DB+RT) belonging to one of C-Schule school flights.

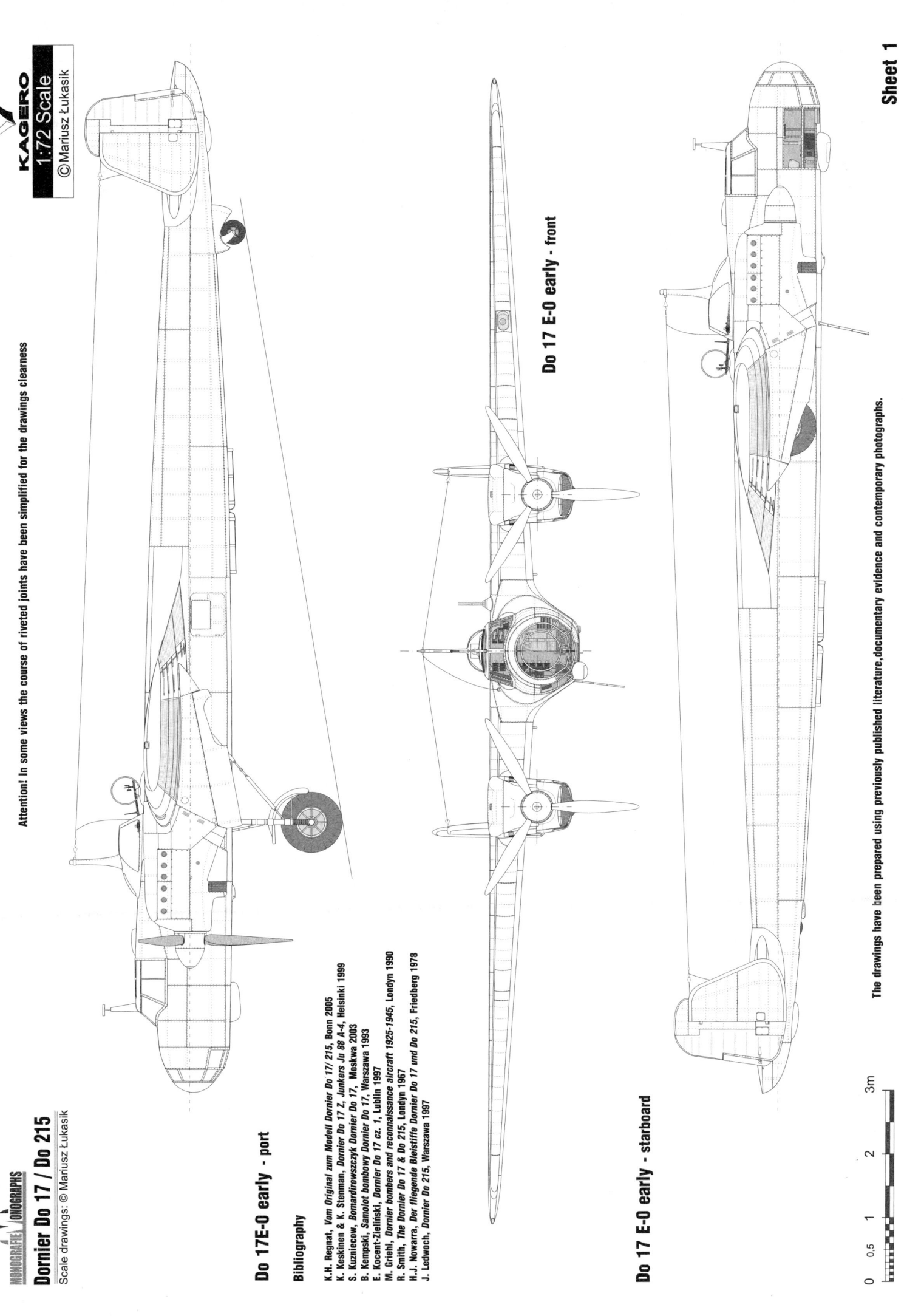

MONOGRAFIE / MONOGRAPHS
Dornier Do 17 / Do 215
Scale drawings: © Mariusz Łukasik

KAGERO
1:72 Scale
© Mariusz Łukasik

Sheet 1

Attention! In some views the course of riveted joints have been simplified for the drawings clearness

Do 17 E-0 early - front

Do 17 E-0 early - port

Do 17 E-0 early - starboard

Bibliography

K.H. Regnat, *Vom Original zum Modell Dornier Do 17/ 215*, Bonn 2005
K. Keskinen & K. Stenman, *Dornier Do 17 Z, Junkers Ju 88 A-4*, Helsinki 1999
S. Kuzniecow, *Bombardirowszczyk Dornier Do 17*, Moskwa 2003
B. Kempski, *Samolot bombowy Dornier Do 17*, Warszawa 1993
E. Kocent-Zieliński, *Dornier Do 17 cz. 1*, Lublin 1997
M. Griehl, *Dornier bombers and reconnaissance aircraft 1925-1945*, Londyn 1990
R. Smith, *The Dornier Do 17 & Do 215*, Londyn 1967
H.J. Nowarra, *Der fliegende Bleistifte Dornier Do 17 und Do 215*, Friedberg 1978
J. Ledwoch, *Dornier Do 215*, Warszawa 1997

The drawings have been prepared using previously published literature, documentary evidence and contemporary photographs.

0   0,5   1   2   3m

KAGERO

1:72 Scale

©Mariusz Łukasik

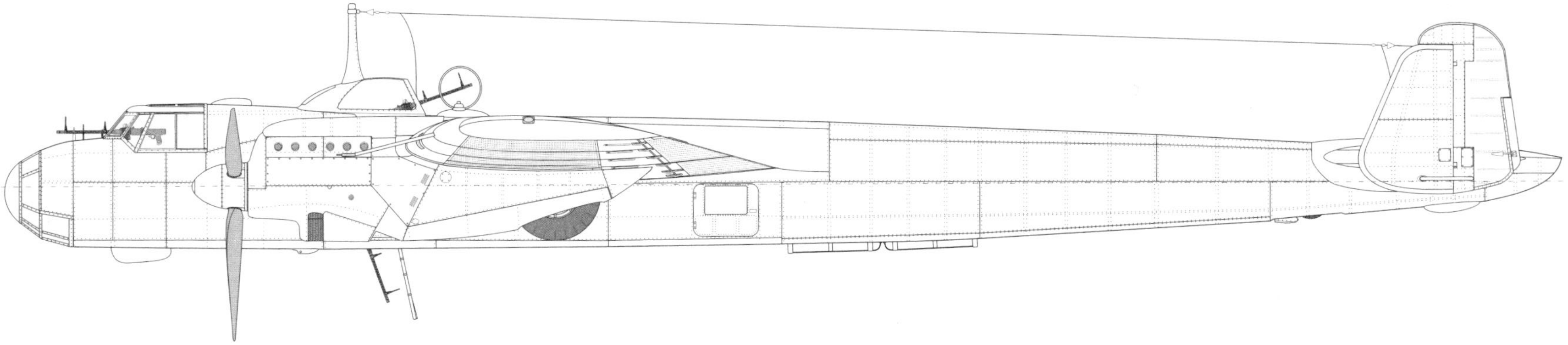

MONOGRAFIE MONOGRAPHS

Dornier Do 17 / Do 215

Scale drawings: © Mariusz Łukasik

Do 17 E-1 - port

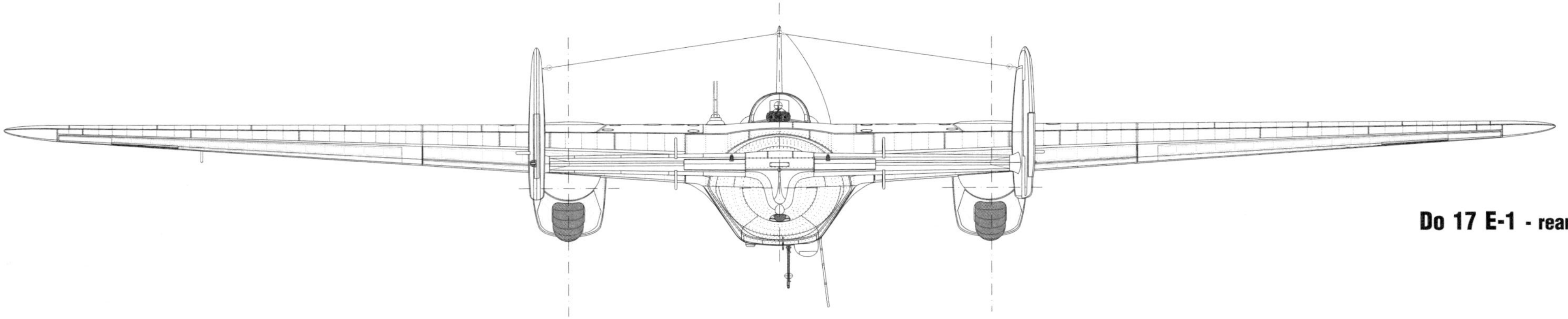

Do 17 E-1 - rear

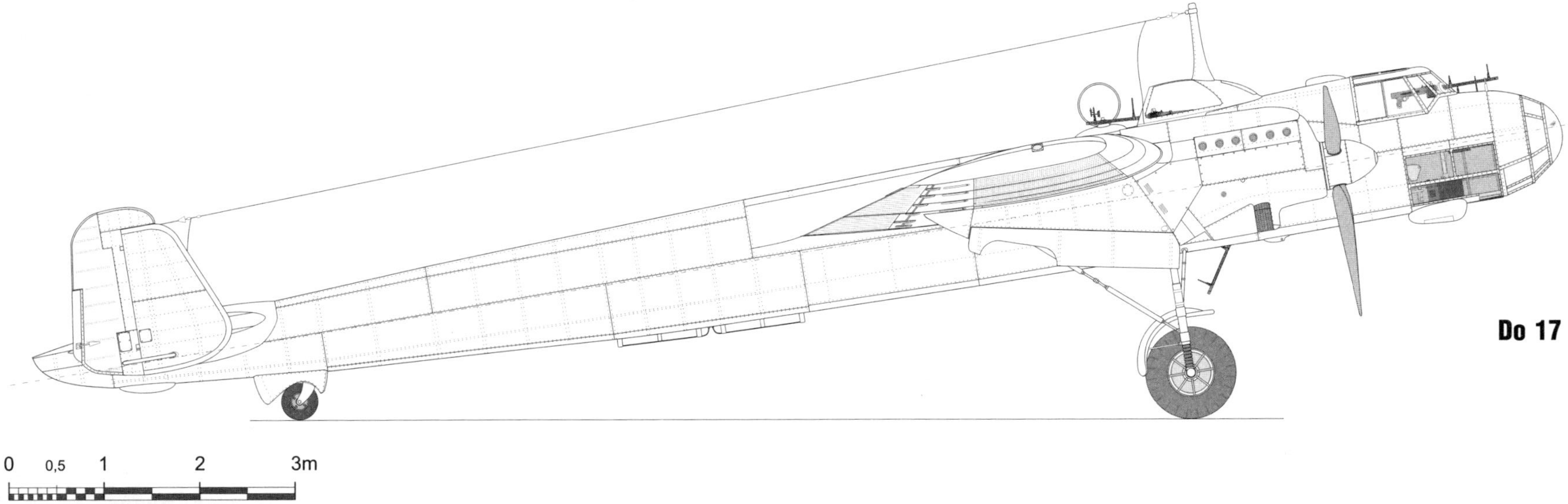

Do 17 E-1 - starboard

Sheet 2

0   0.5   1   2   3m

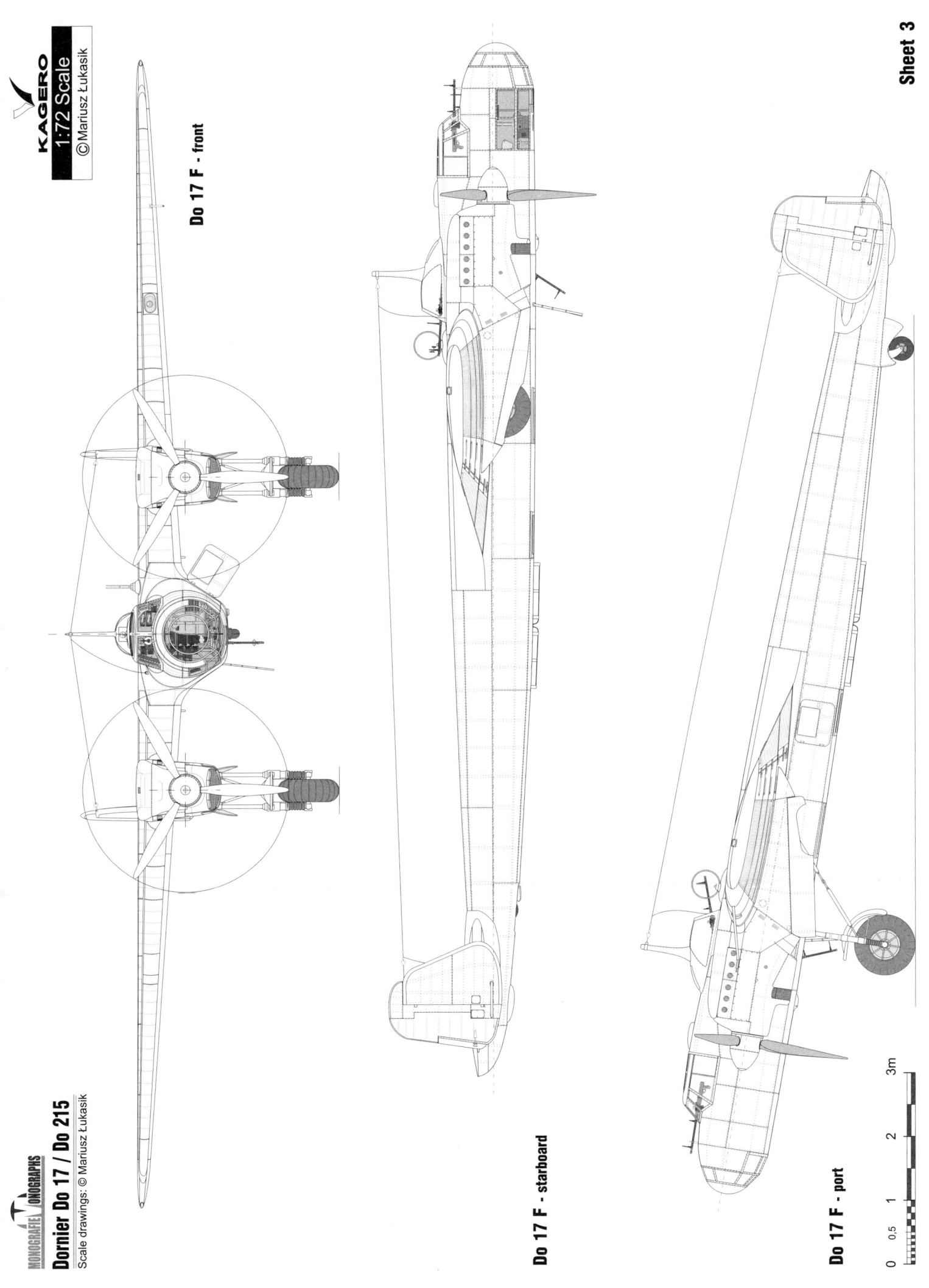

MONOGRAFIE MONOGRAPHS
Dornier Do 17 / Do 215
Scale drawings: © Mariusz Łukasik

KAGERO
1:72 Scale
© Mariusz Łukasik

Do 17 F - front

Do 17 F - starboard

Do 17 F - port

Sheet 3

0   0,5   1   2   3m

KAGERO
1:72 Scale
© Mariusz Łukasik

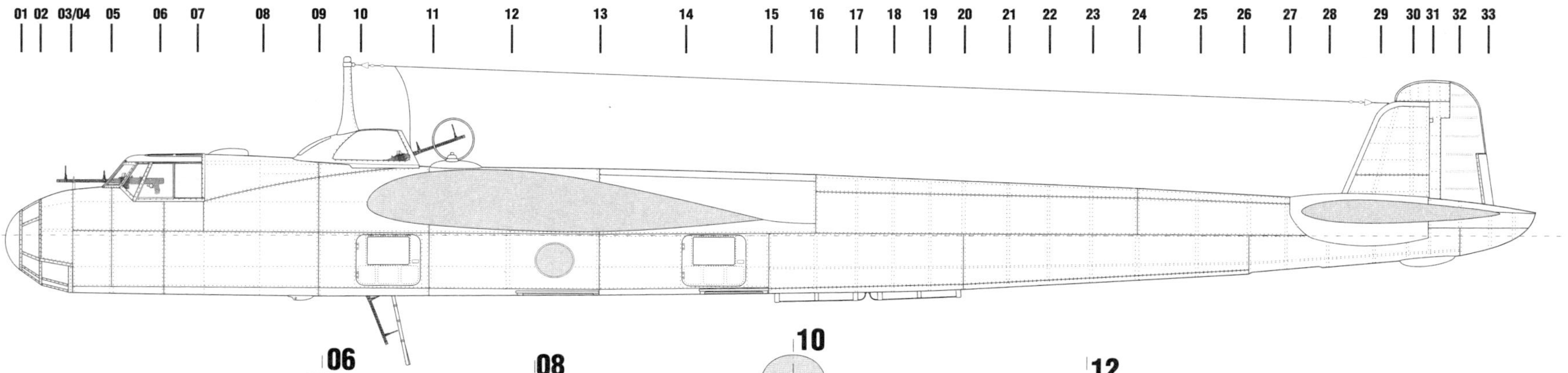

MONOGRAFIE/MONOGRAPHS
Dornier Do 17 / Do 215
Scale drawings: © Mariusz Łukasik

01 02 03/04 05 06 07 08 09 10 11 12 13 14 15 16 17 18 19 20 21 22 23 24 25 26 27 28 29 30 31 32 33

Do 17 F - port

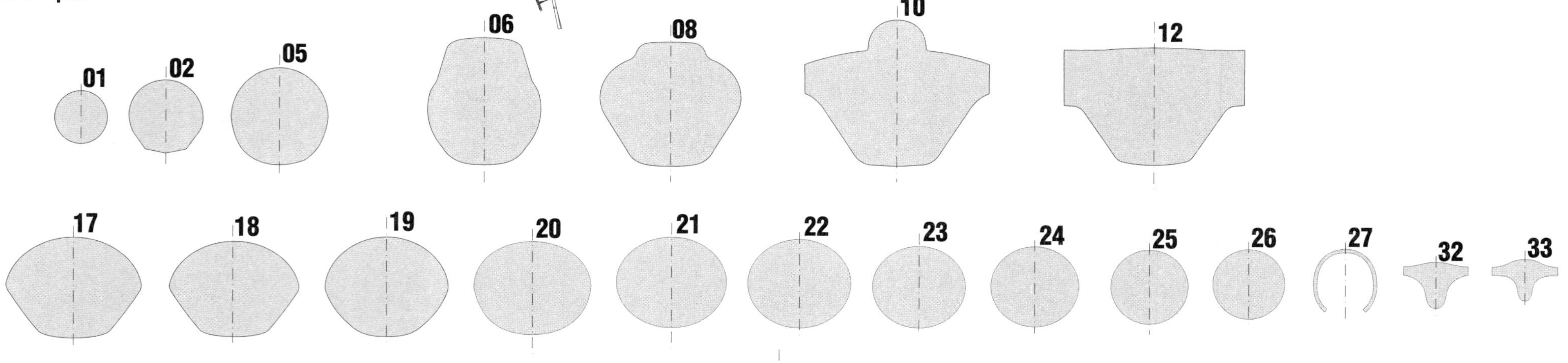

01 02 05 06 08 10 12

17 18 19 20 21 22 23 24 25 26 27 32 33

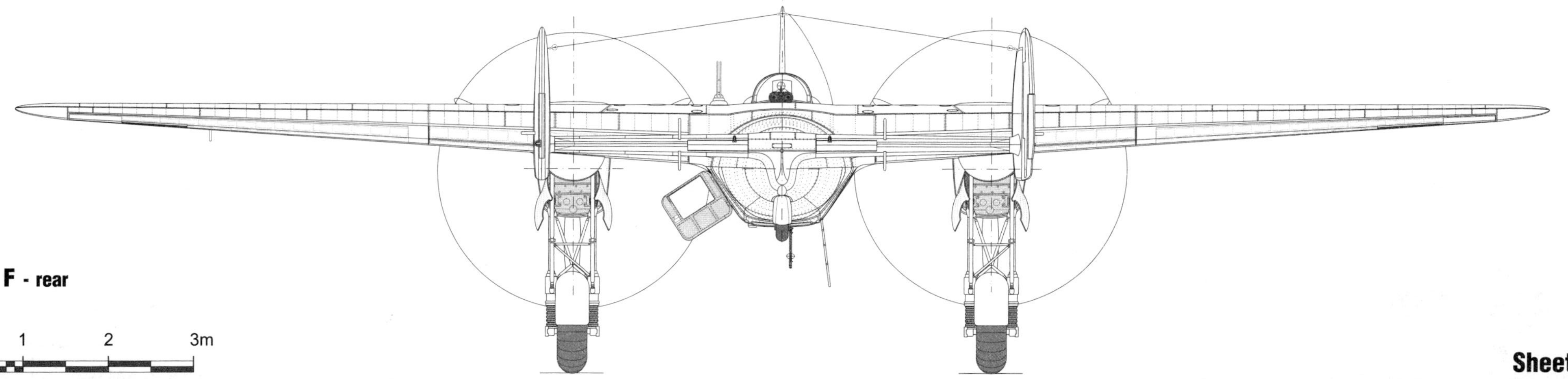

Do 17 F - rear

0   0,5   1   2   3m

Sheet 4

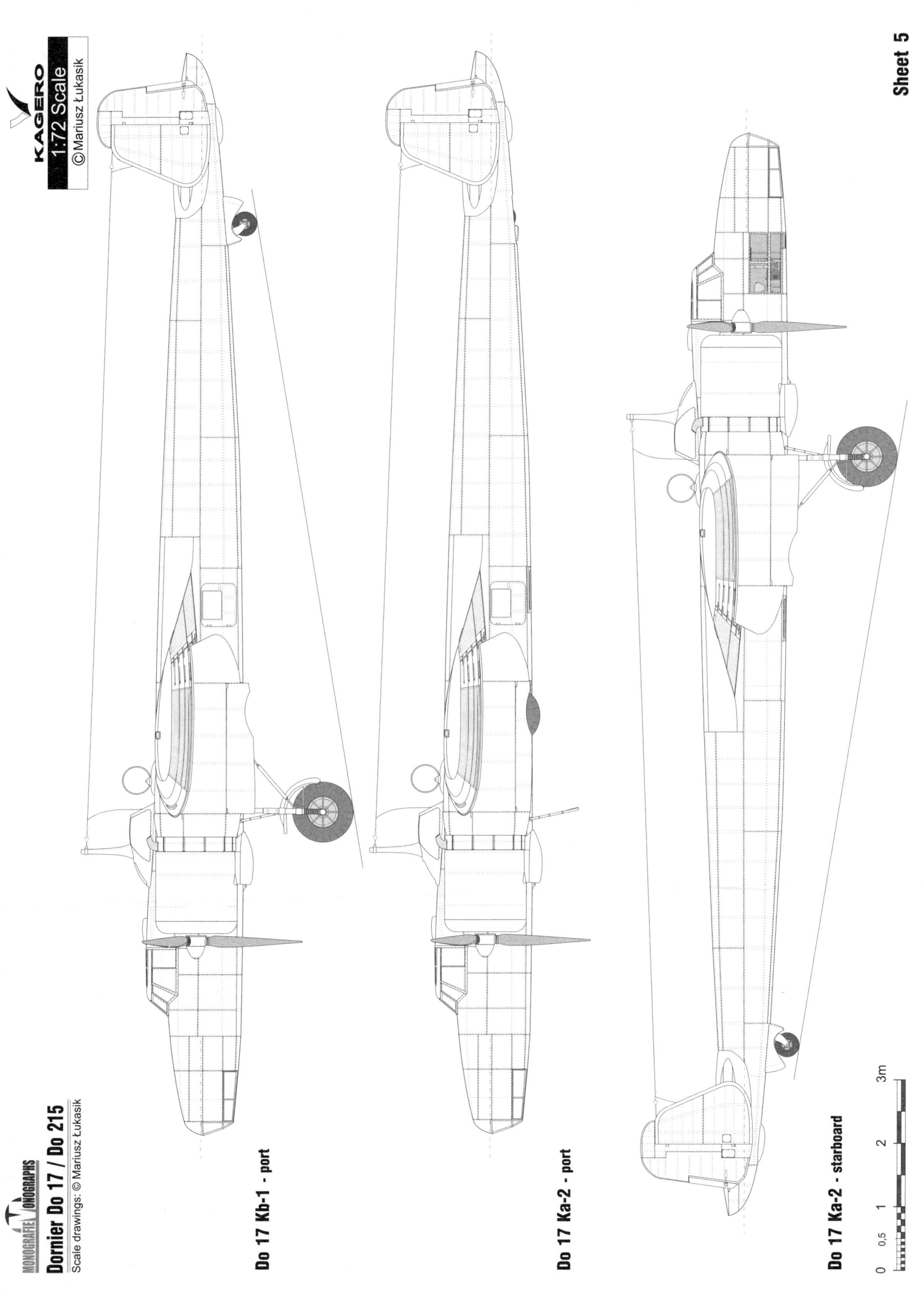

MONOGRAFIE MONOGRAPHS
Dornier Do 17 / Do 215
Scale drawings: © Mariusz Łukasik

KAGERO
1:72 Scale
©Mariusz Łukasik

Do 17 Kb-1 - port

Do 17 Ka-2 - port

Do 17 Ka-2 - starboard

Sheet 5

0 0,5 1 2 3m

KAGERO
1:72 Scale
©Mariusz Łukasik

MONOGRAFIE MONOGRAPHS
Dornier Do 17 / Do 215
Scale drawings: © Mariusz Łukasik

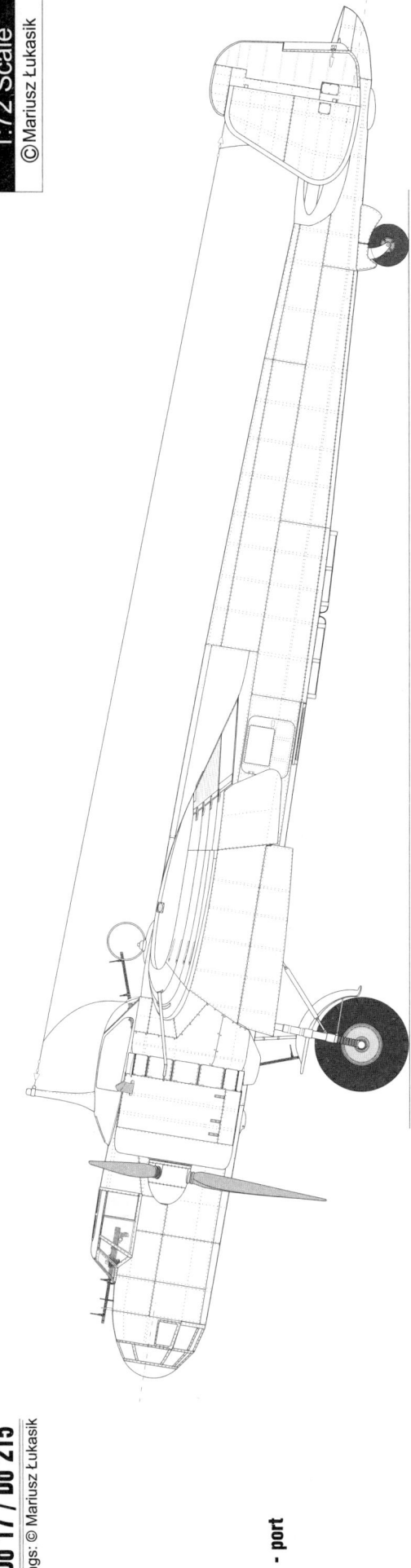

Do 17 P - port

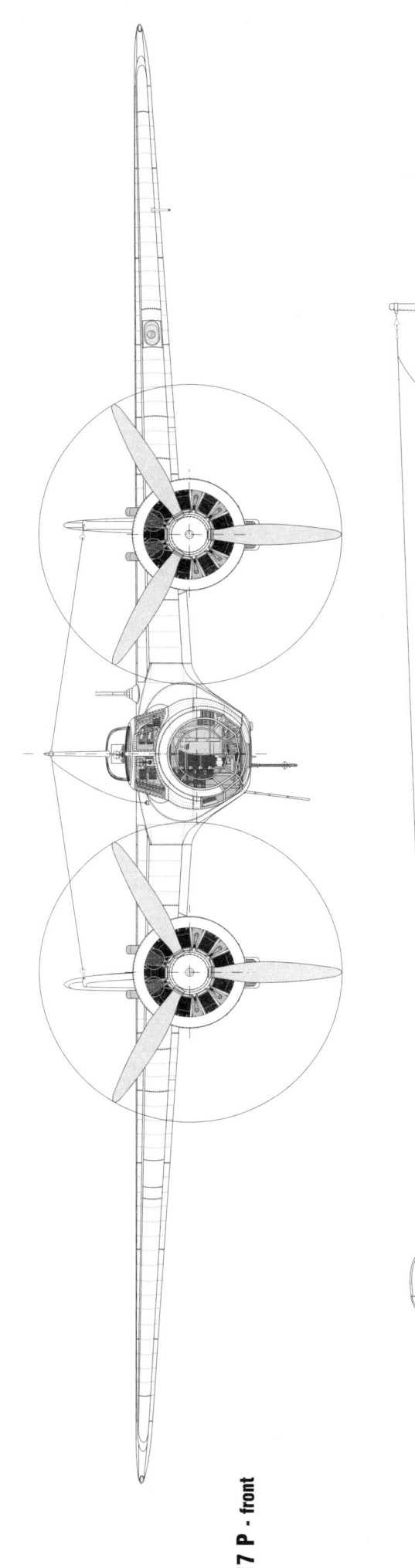

Do 17 P - front

Do 17 P - starboard

Sheet 6

0   0,5   1   2   3m

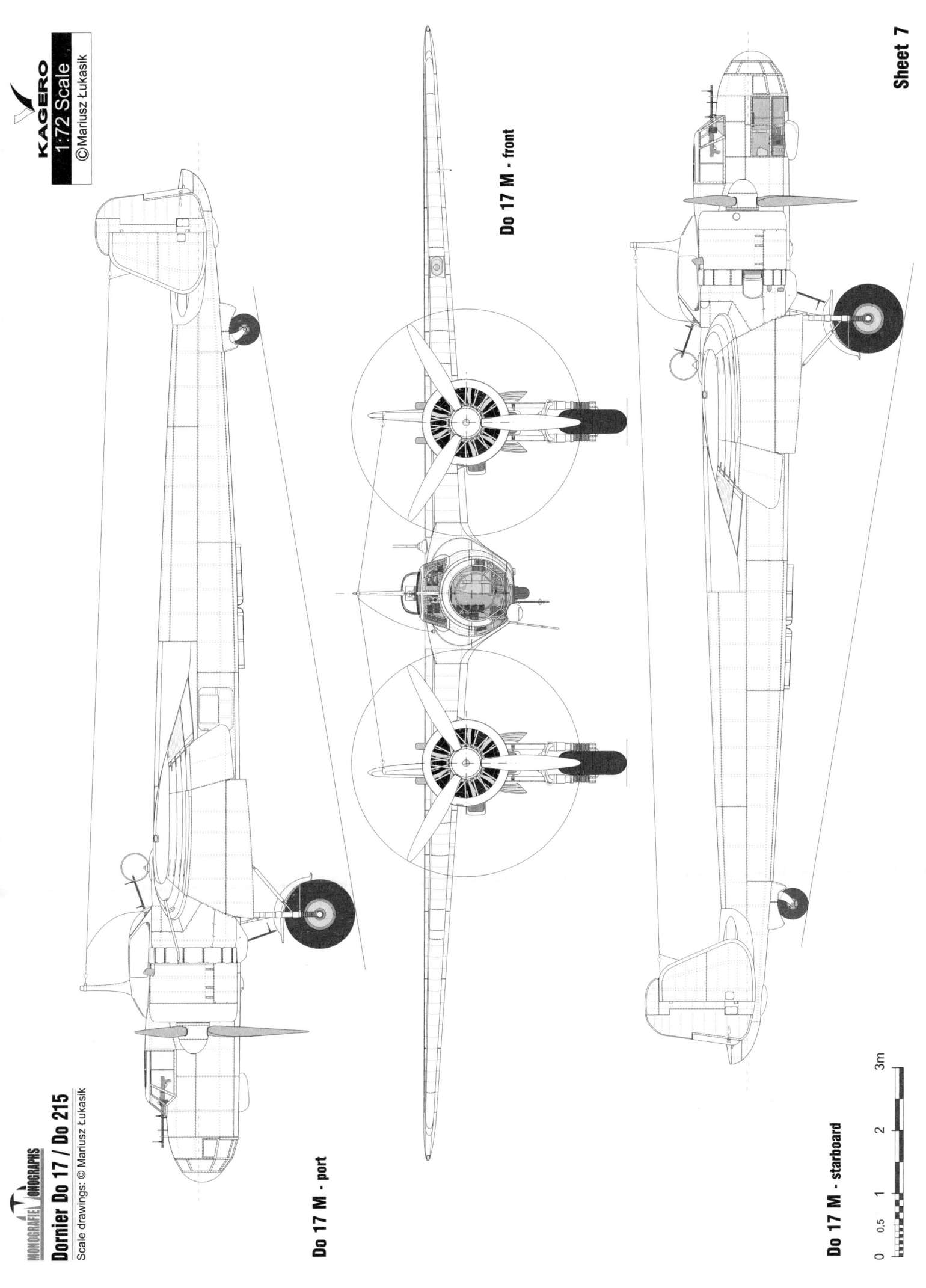

Dornier Do 17 / Do 215

Scale drawings: © Mariusz Łukasik

1:72 Scale

© Mariusz Łukasik

Do 17 M - front

Do 17 M - port

Do 17 M - starboard

Sheet 7

0   0,5   1   2   3m

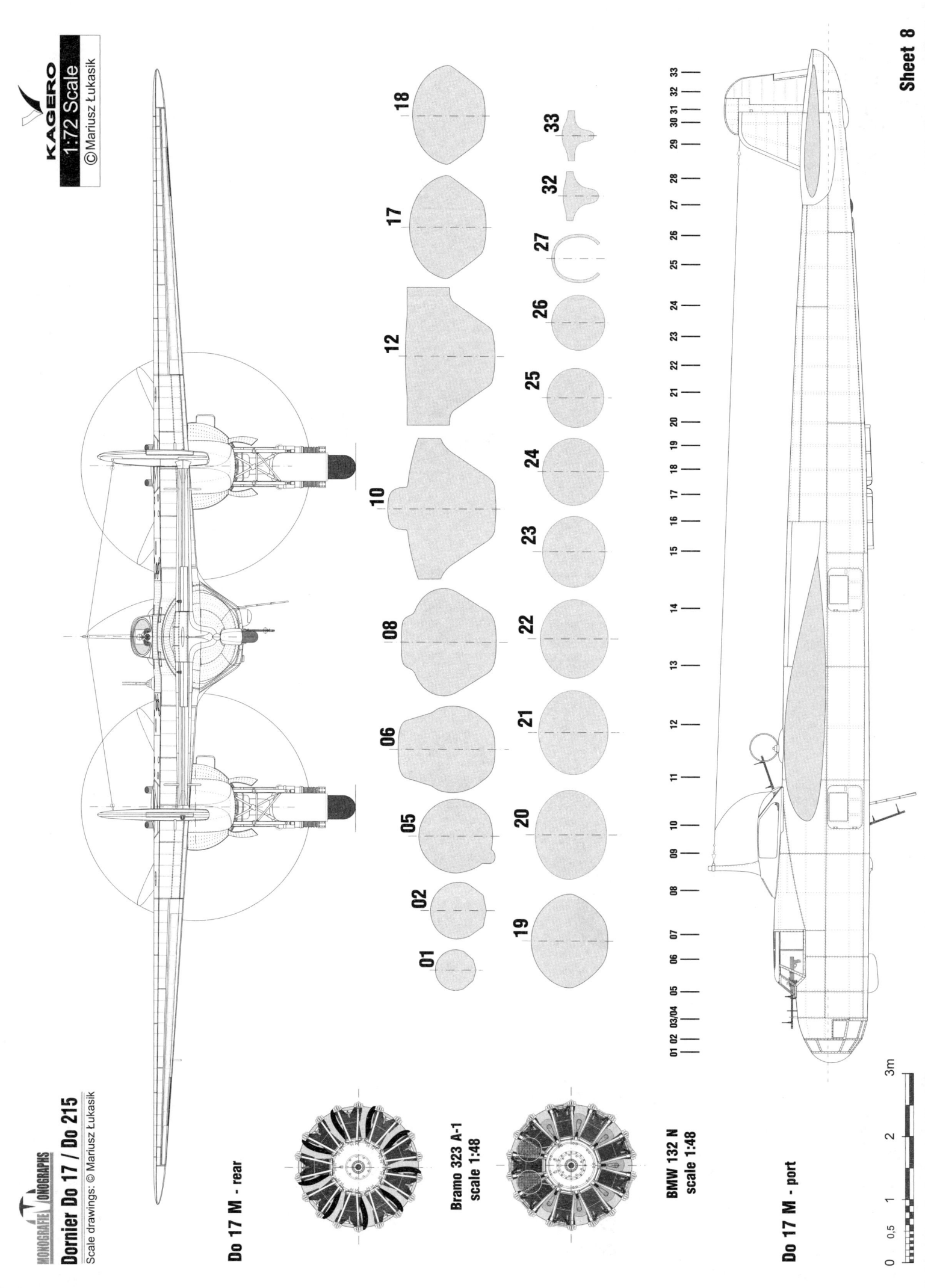

KAGERO

MONOGRAFIE MONOGRAPHS
Dornier Do 17 / Do 215
Scale drawings: © Mariusz Łukasik

1:72 Scale
© Mariusz Łukasik

Sheet 8

Do 17 M - rear

Bramo 323 A-1
scale 1:48

BMW 132 N
scale 1:48

Do 17 M - port

0   0,5   1   2   3m

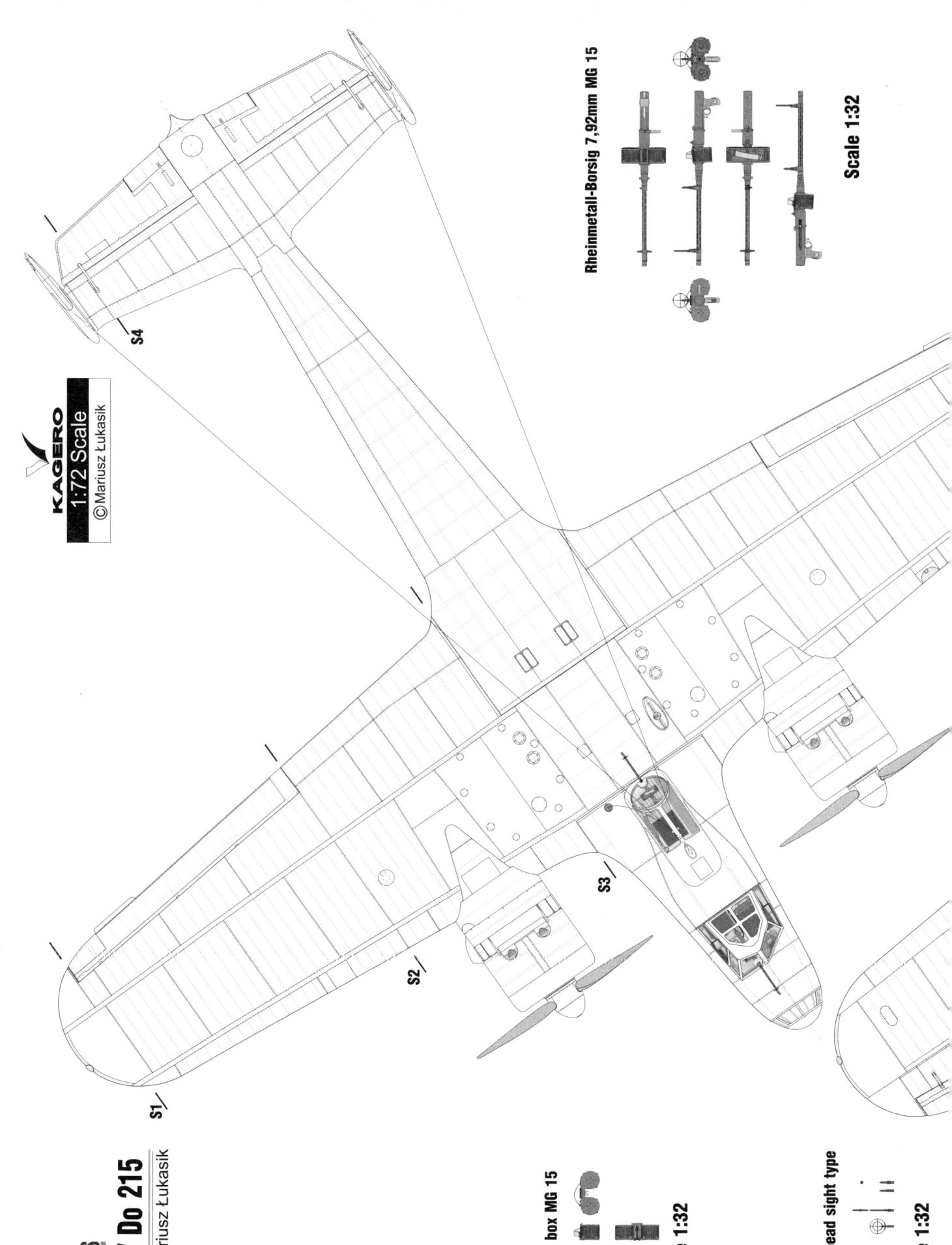

MONOGRAFIE MONOGRAPHS

Dornier Do 17 / Do 215

Scale drawings: © Mariusz Łukasik

Do 17 M - top

KAGERO
1:72 Scale
©Mariusz Łukasik

Rheinmetall-Borsig 7,92mm MG 15

Scale 1:32

Ammunition box MG 15

Scale 1:32

Ring-and-bead sight type

Scale 1:32

S1

S2

S3

S4

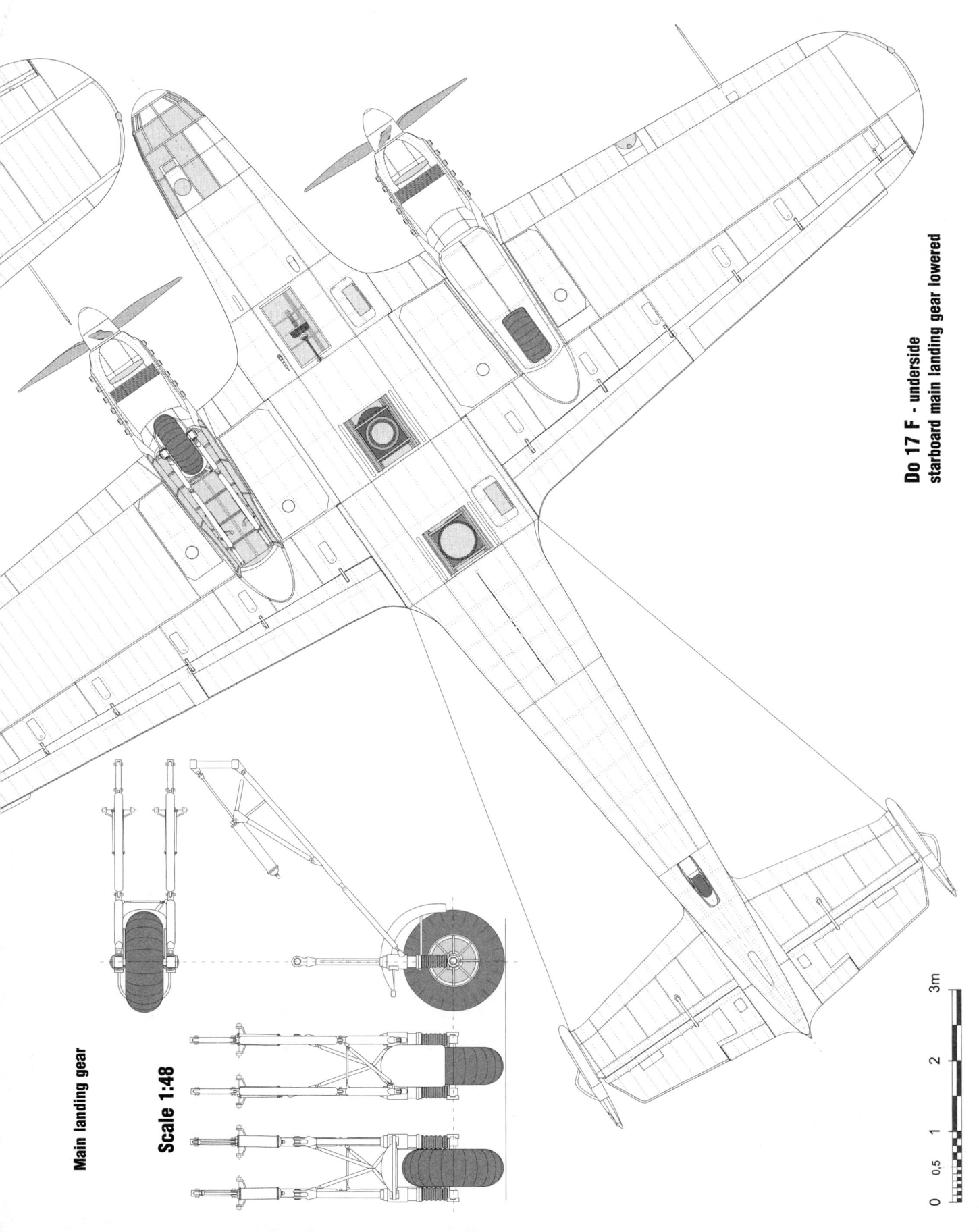

Main landing gear

Scale 1:48

Sheet A

Do 17 F - underside
starboard main landing gear lowered

0   0,5   1   2   3m

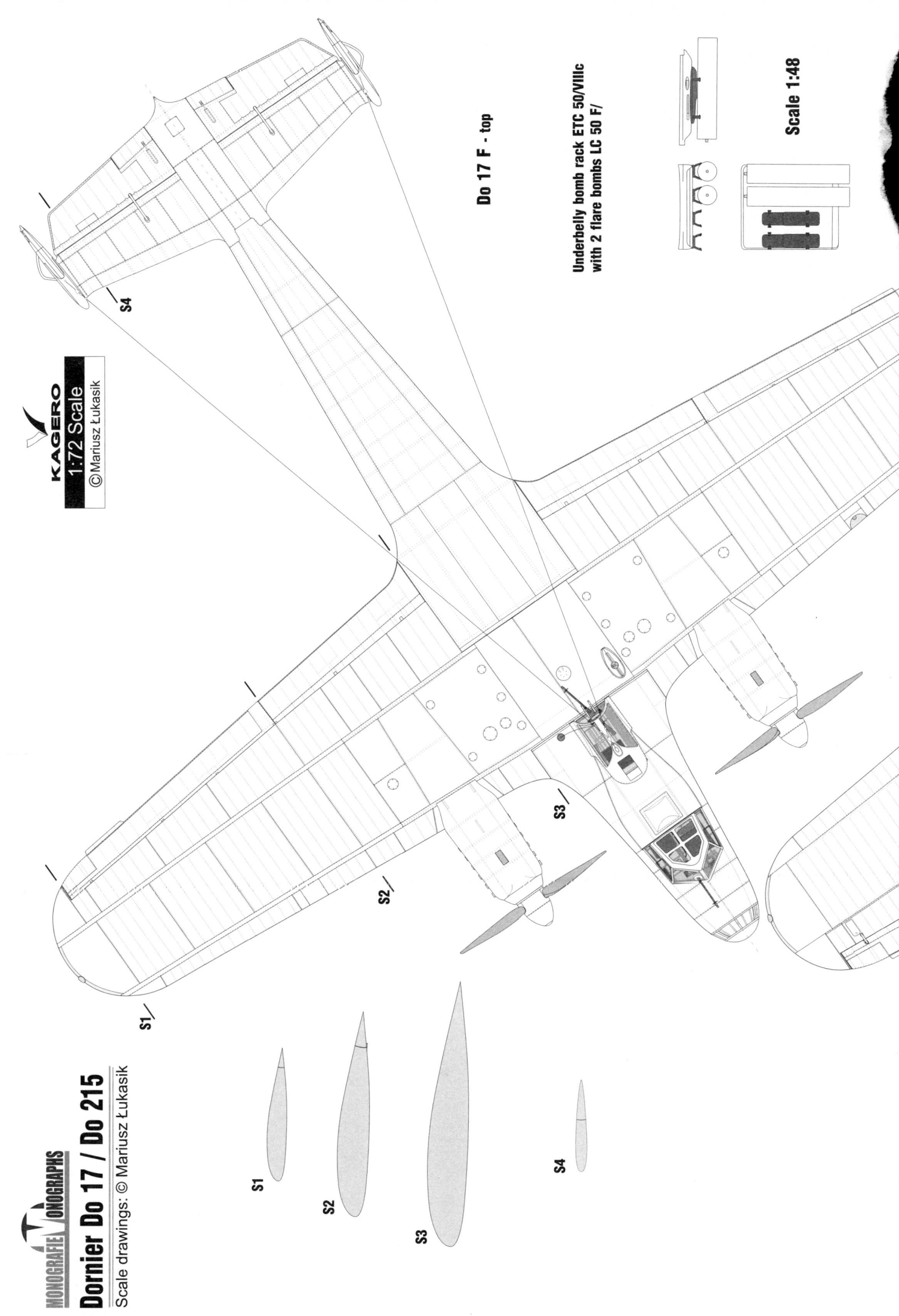

MONOGRAFIE MONOGRAPHS

Dornier Do 17 / Do 215

Scale drawings: © Mariusz Łukasik

KAGERO
1:72 Scale
© Mariusz Łukasik

Do 17 F - top

Underbelly bomb rack ETC 50/VIIIc
with 2 flare bombs LC 50 F/

Scale 1:48

S1

S2

S3

S4

S1

S2

S3

S4

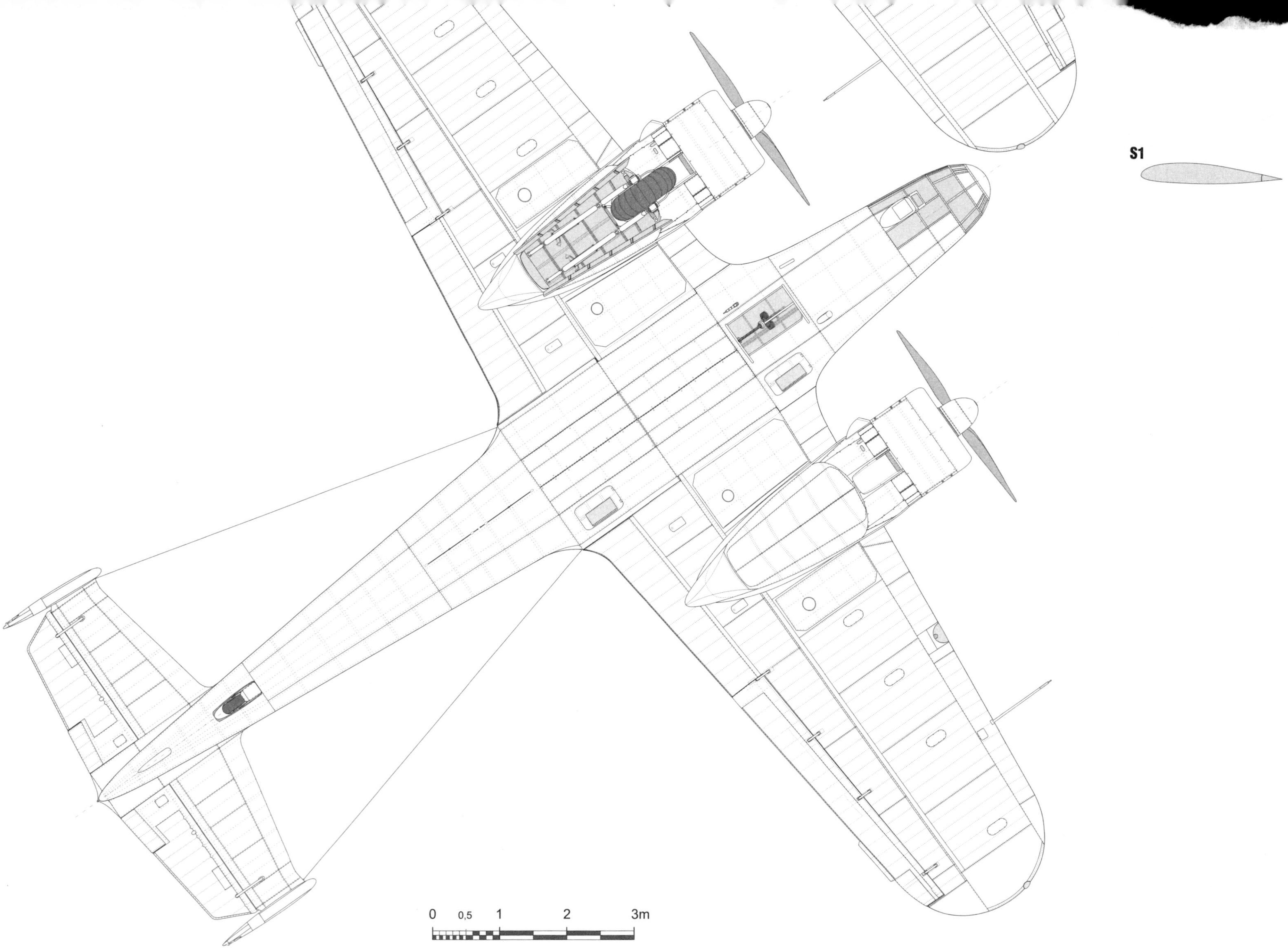

S1

0   0,5   1   2   3m

KAGERO

1:72 Scale

© Mariusz Łukasik

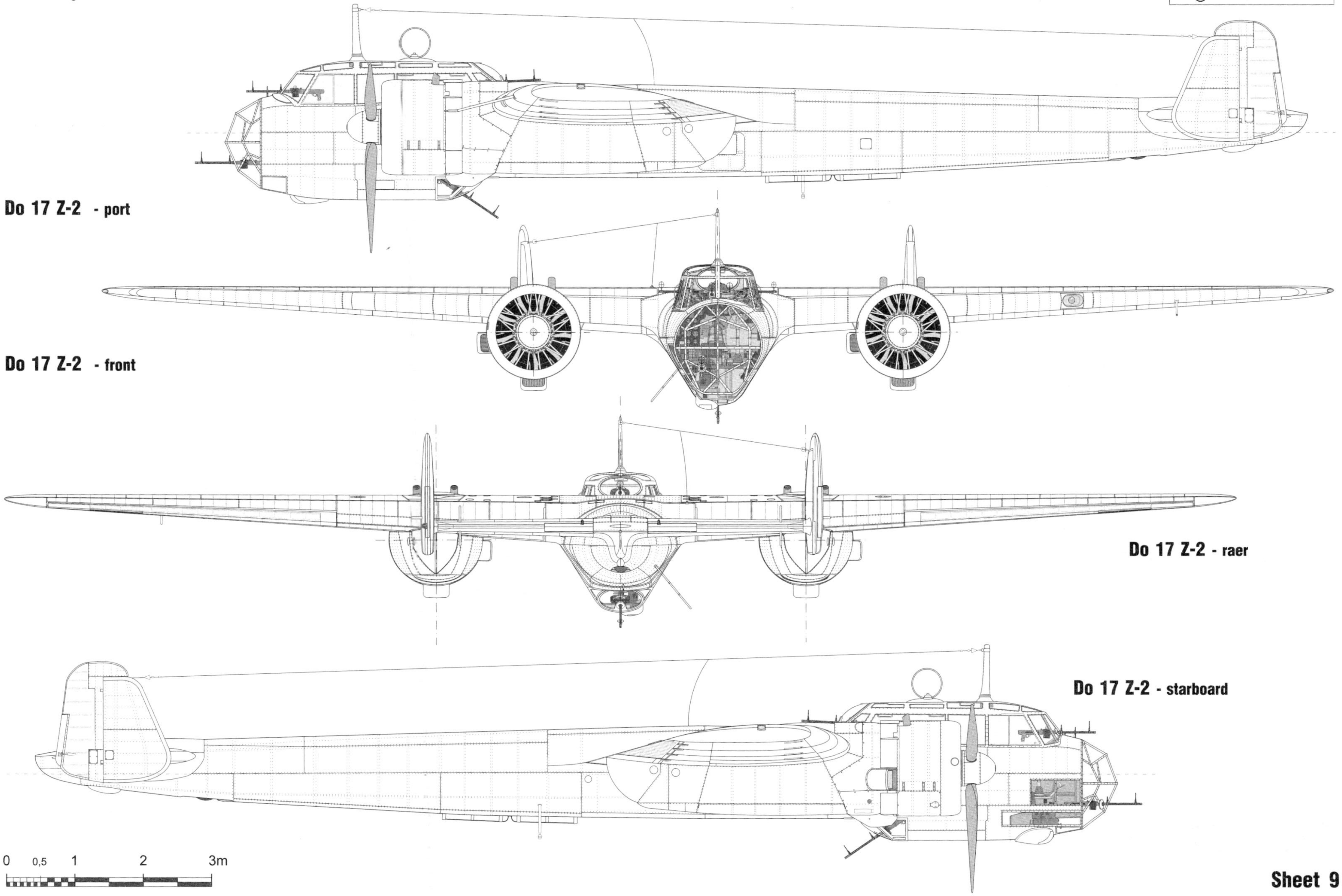

MONOGRAFIE / ONOGRAPHS

Dornier Do 17 / Do 215

Scale drawings: © Mariusz Łukasik

Do 17 Z-2 - port

Do 17 Z-2 - front

Do 17 Z-2 - raer

Do 17 Z-2 - starboard

Sheet 9

0   0,5   1   2   3m

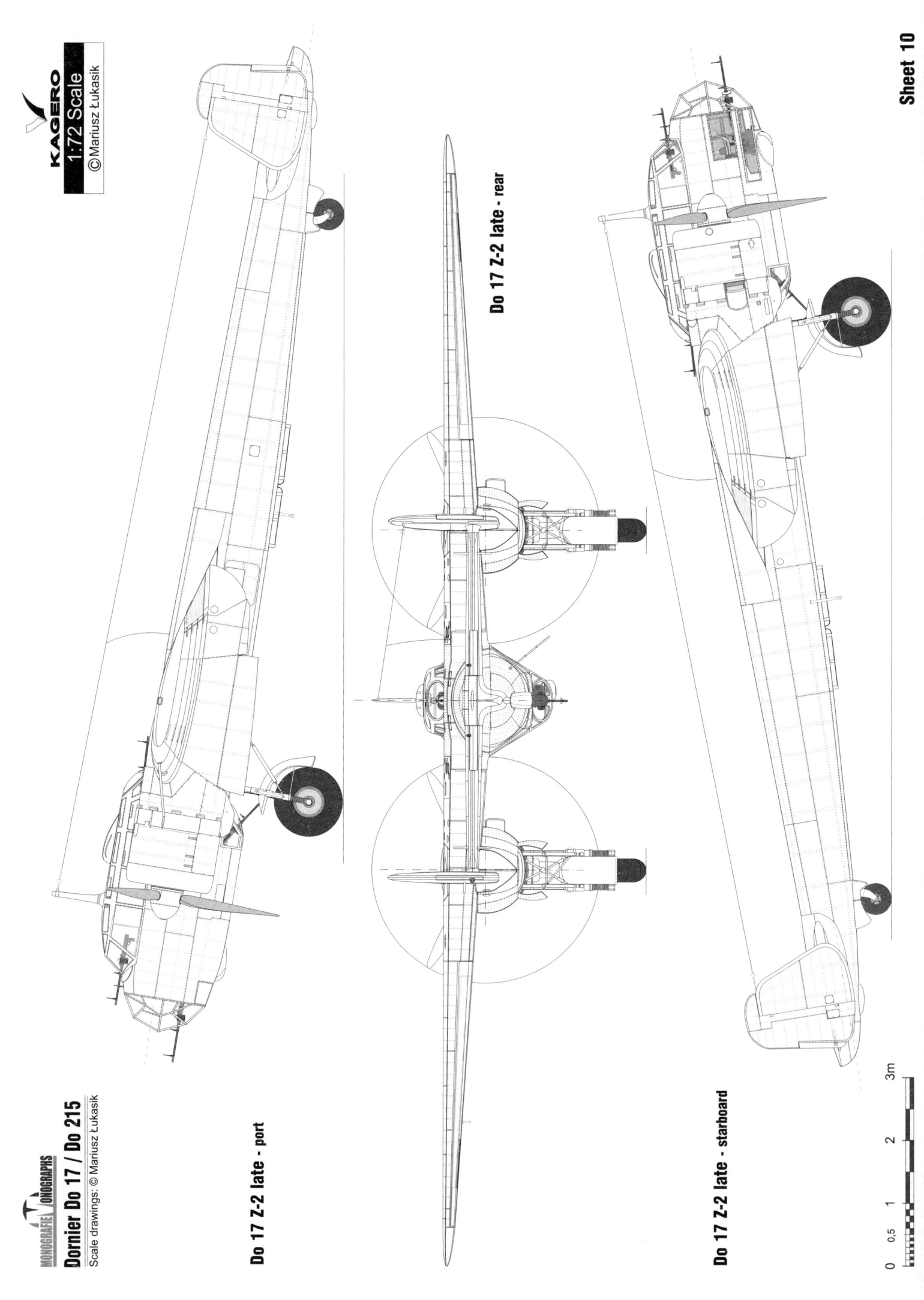

MONOGRAFIE MONOGRAPHS
Dornier Do 17 / Do 215
Scale drawings: ©Mariusz Łukasik

Do 17 Z-2 late - port

Do 17 Z-2 late - rear

Do 17 Z-2 late - starboard

Sheet 10

0   0,5   1   2   3m

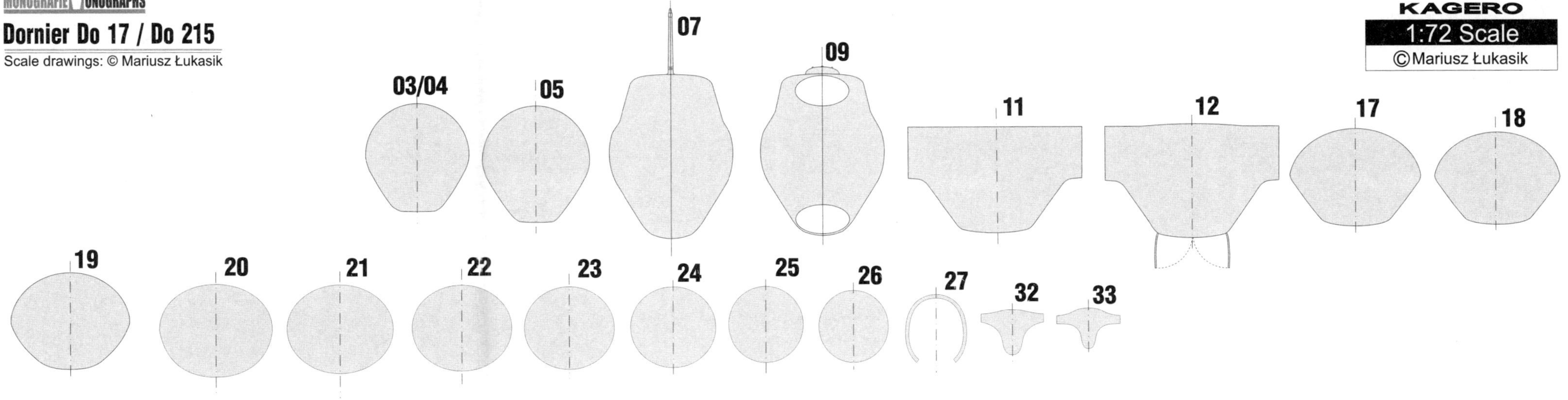

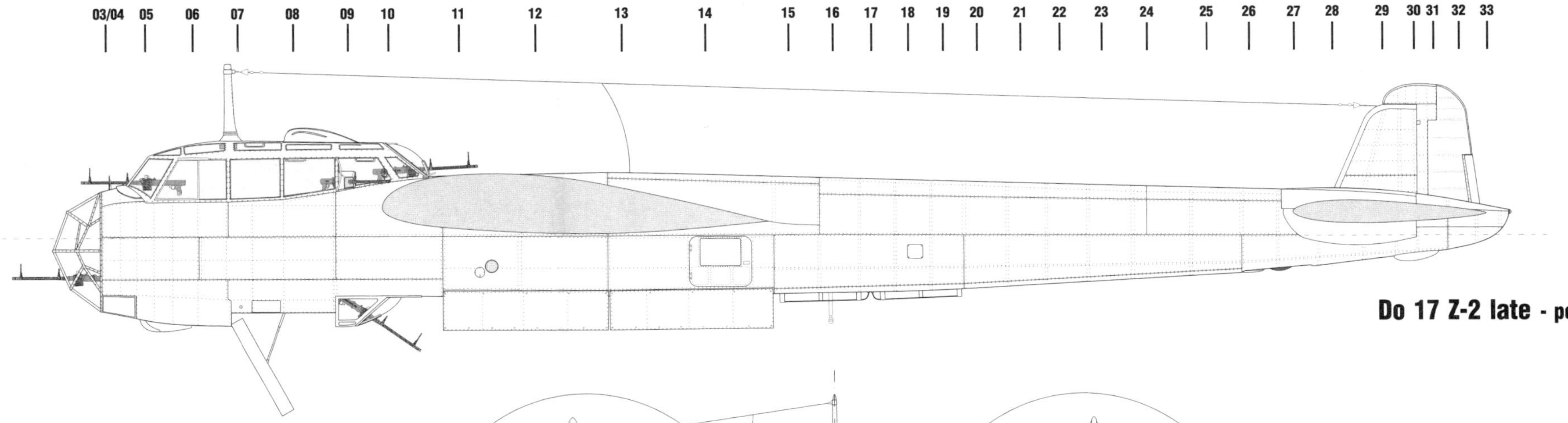

KAGERO

MONOGRAFIE MONOGRAPHS

Dornier Do 17 / Do 215

1:72 Scale

© Mariusz Łukasik

Scale drawings: © Mariusz Łukasik

Do 17 Z-2 late - port

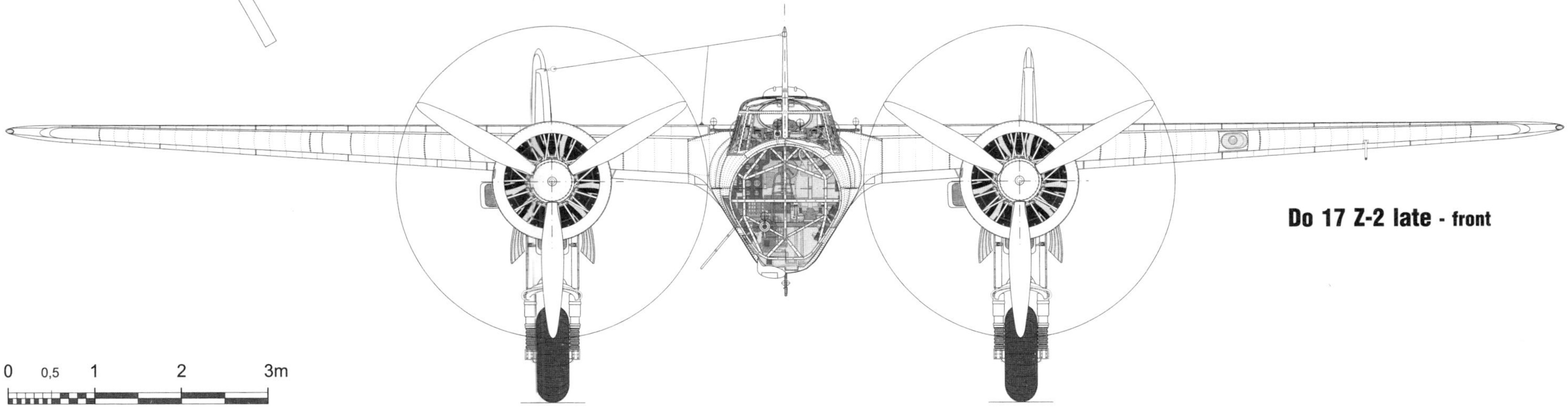

Do 17 Z-2 late - front

Sheet 11

0 0,5 1 2 3m

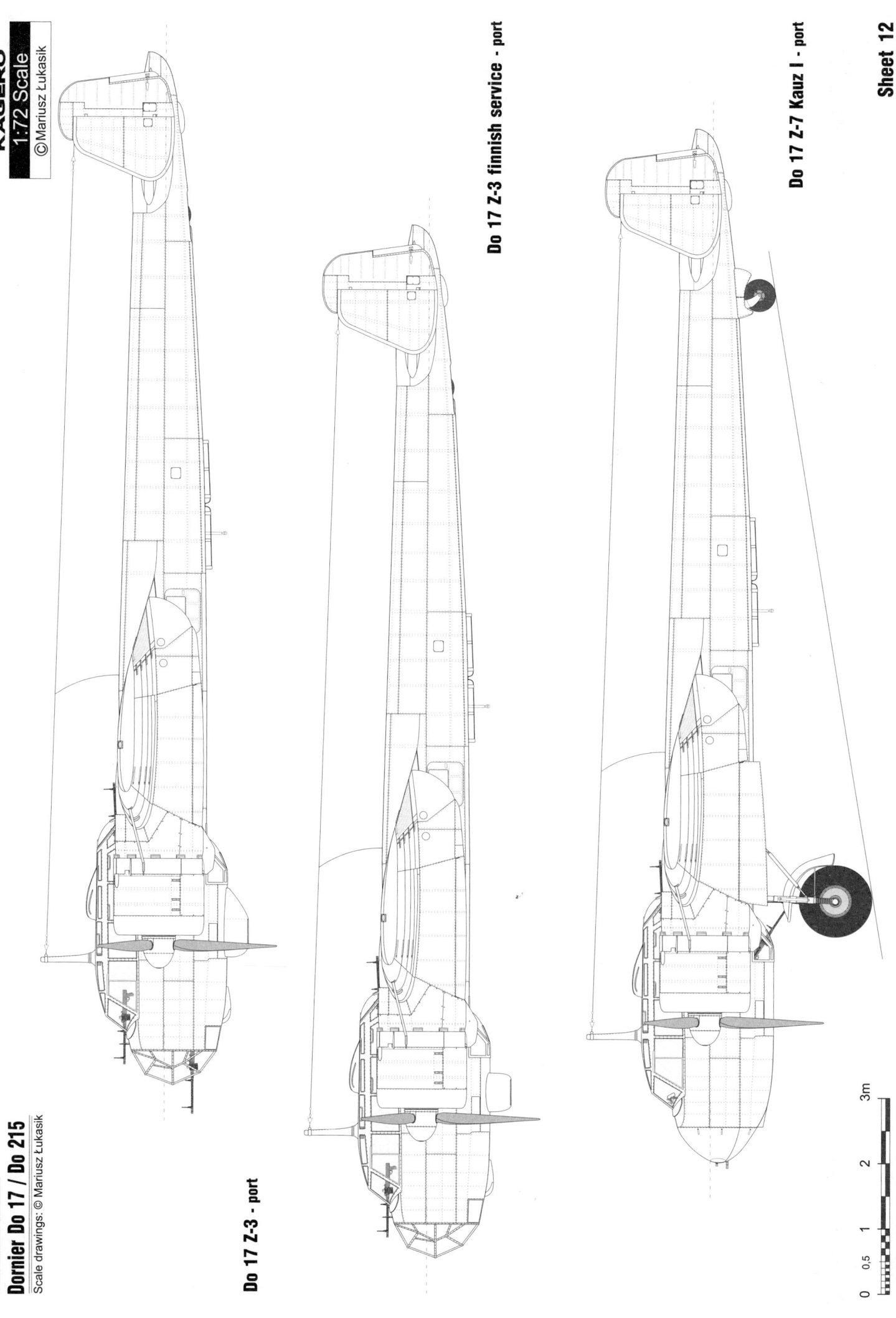

MONOGRAFIE MONOGRAPHS
Dornier Do 17 / Do 215
Scale drawings: © Mariusz Łukasik

KAGERO
1:72 Scale
© Mariusz Łukasik

Do 17 Z-3 - port

Do 17 Z-3 finnish service - port

Do 17 Z-7 Kauz I - port

Sheet 12

0   0,5   1   2   3m

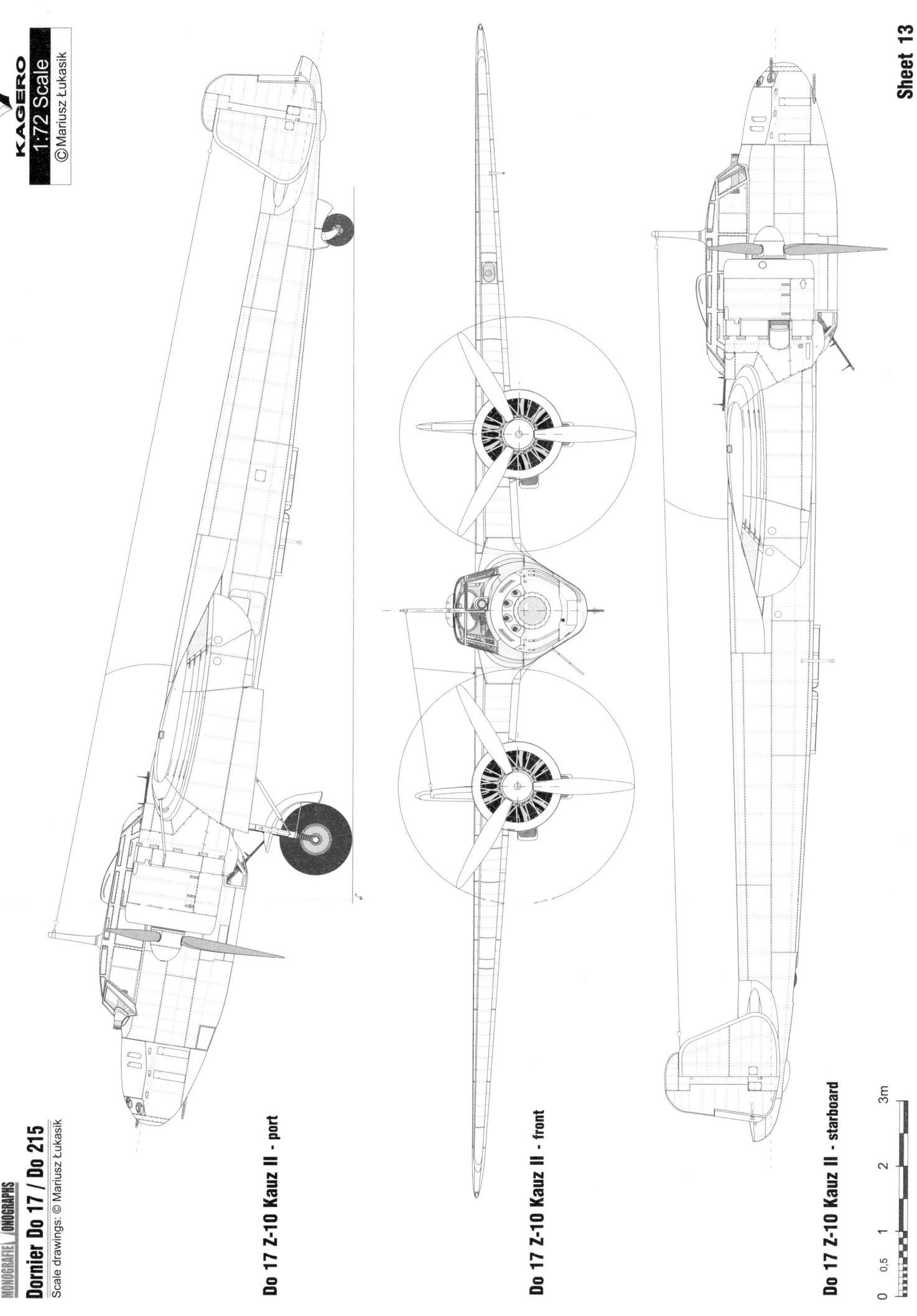

KAGERO
1:72 Scale
Dornier Do 17 / Do 215
© Mariusz Łukasik

MONOGRAFIE LOTNICZE
Dornier Do 17 / Do 215
Scale drawings: © Mariusz Łukasik

Do 17 Z-10 Kauz II - port

Do 17 Z-10 Kauz II - front

Do 17 Z-10 Kauz II - starboard

Sheet 13

0   0,5   1   2   3m

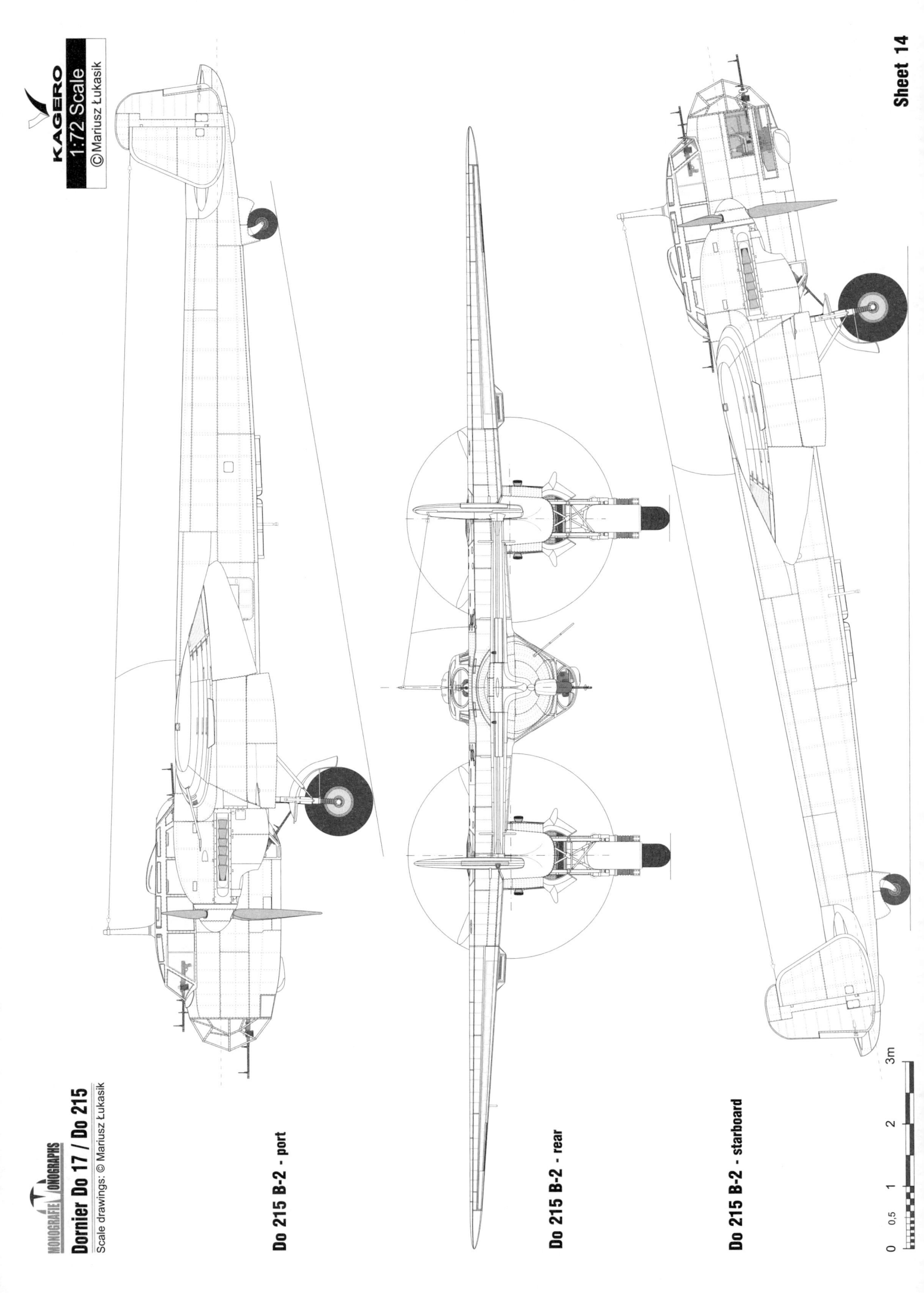

MONOGRAFIE/MONOGRAPHS
Dornier Do 17 / Do 215
Scale drawings: © Mariusz Łukasik

Do 215 B-2 - port

Do 215 B-2 - rear

Do 215 B-2 - starboard

0   0.5   1   2   3m

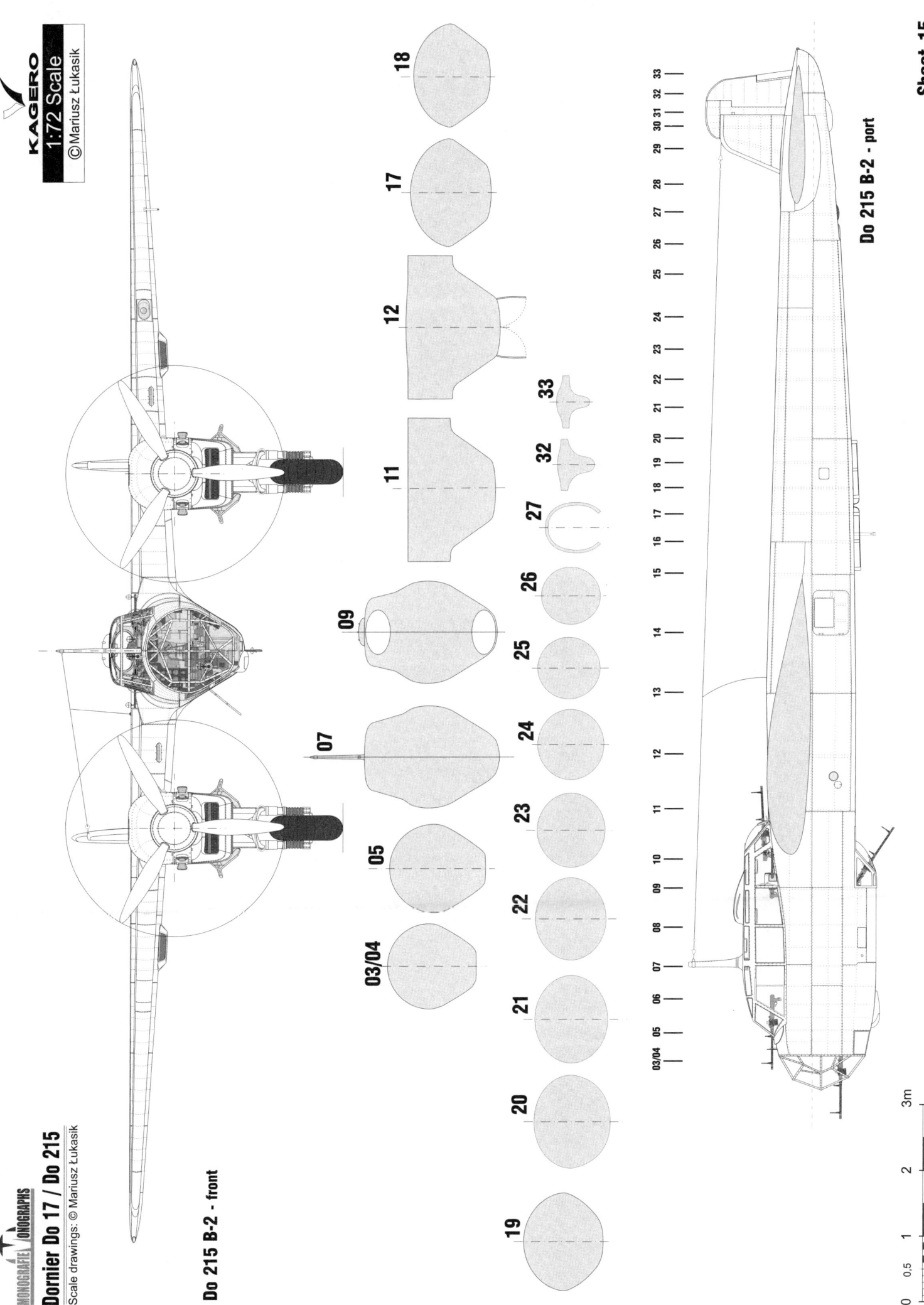

MONOGRAFIE MONOGRAPHS

Dornier Do 17 / Do 215

Scale drawings: © Mariusz Łukasik

KAGERO
1:72 Scale
© Mariusz Łukasik

Do 215 B-2 - front

Do 215 B-2 - port

Sheet 15

0   0,5   1   2   3m

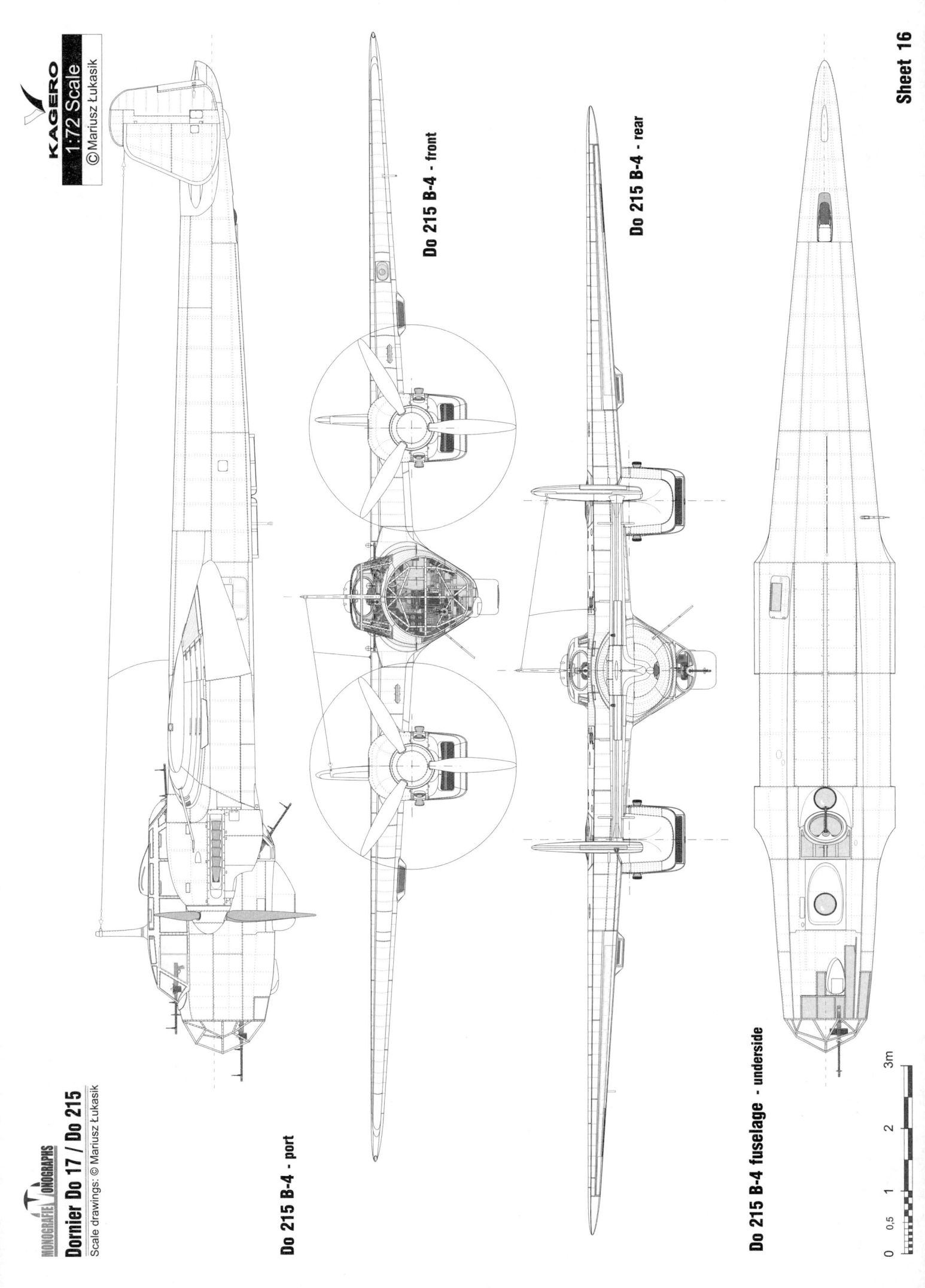

KAGERO

MONOGRAFIE MONOGRAPHS
Dornier Do 17 / Do 215
Scale drawings: © Mariusz Łukasik

1:72 Scale
© Mariusz Łukasik

Do 215 B-4 - front

Do 215 B-4 - rear

Do 215 B-4 - port

Do 215 B-4 fuselage - underside

Sheet 16

0   0,5   1   2   3m

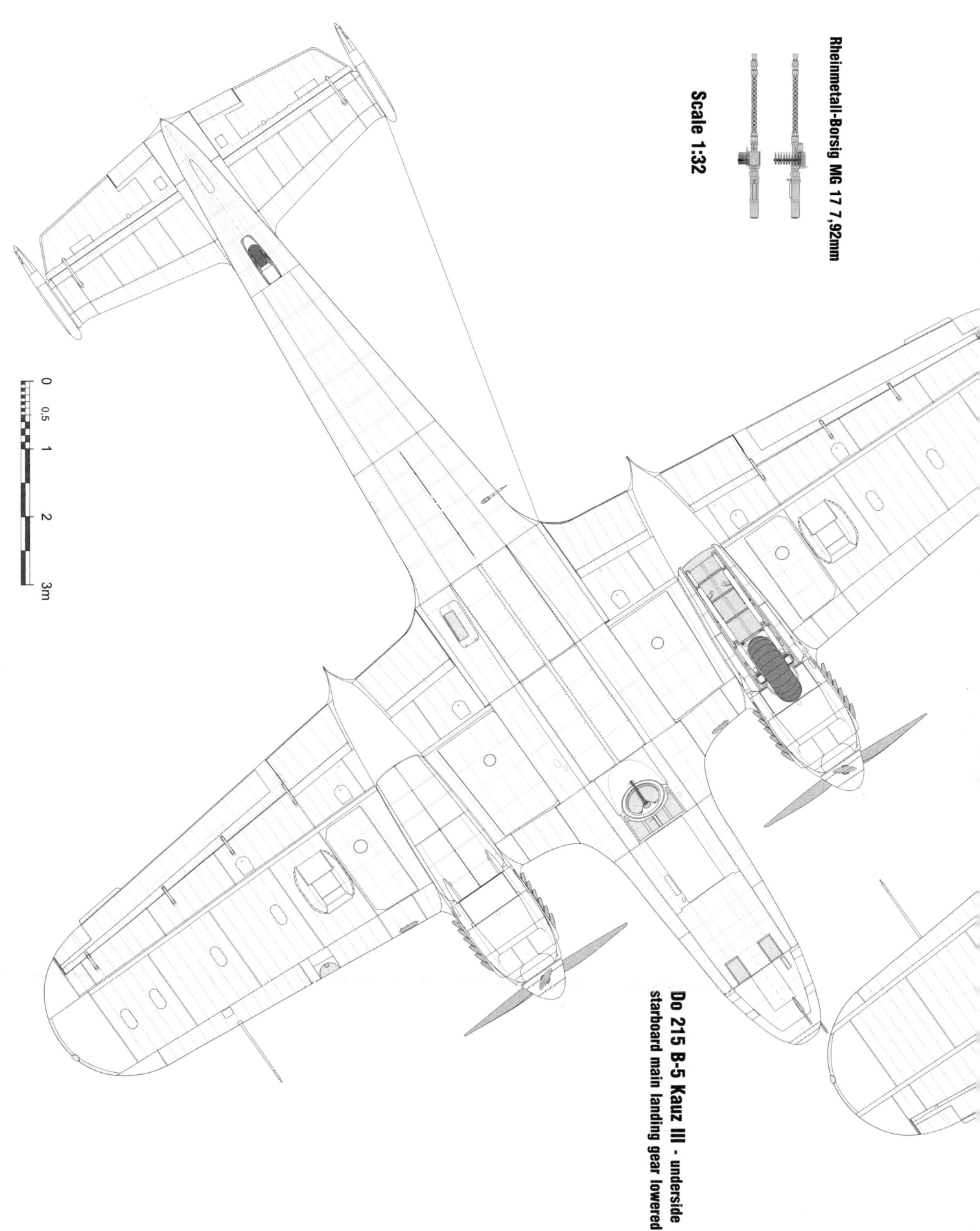

Rheinmetall-Borsig MG 17 7,92mm

Scale 1:32

0 0,5 1 2 3m

Do 215 B-5 Kauz III - underside
starboard main landing gear lowered

Sheet D

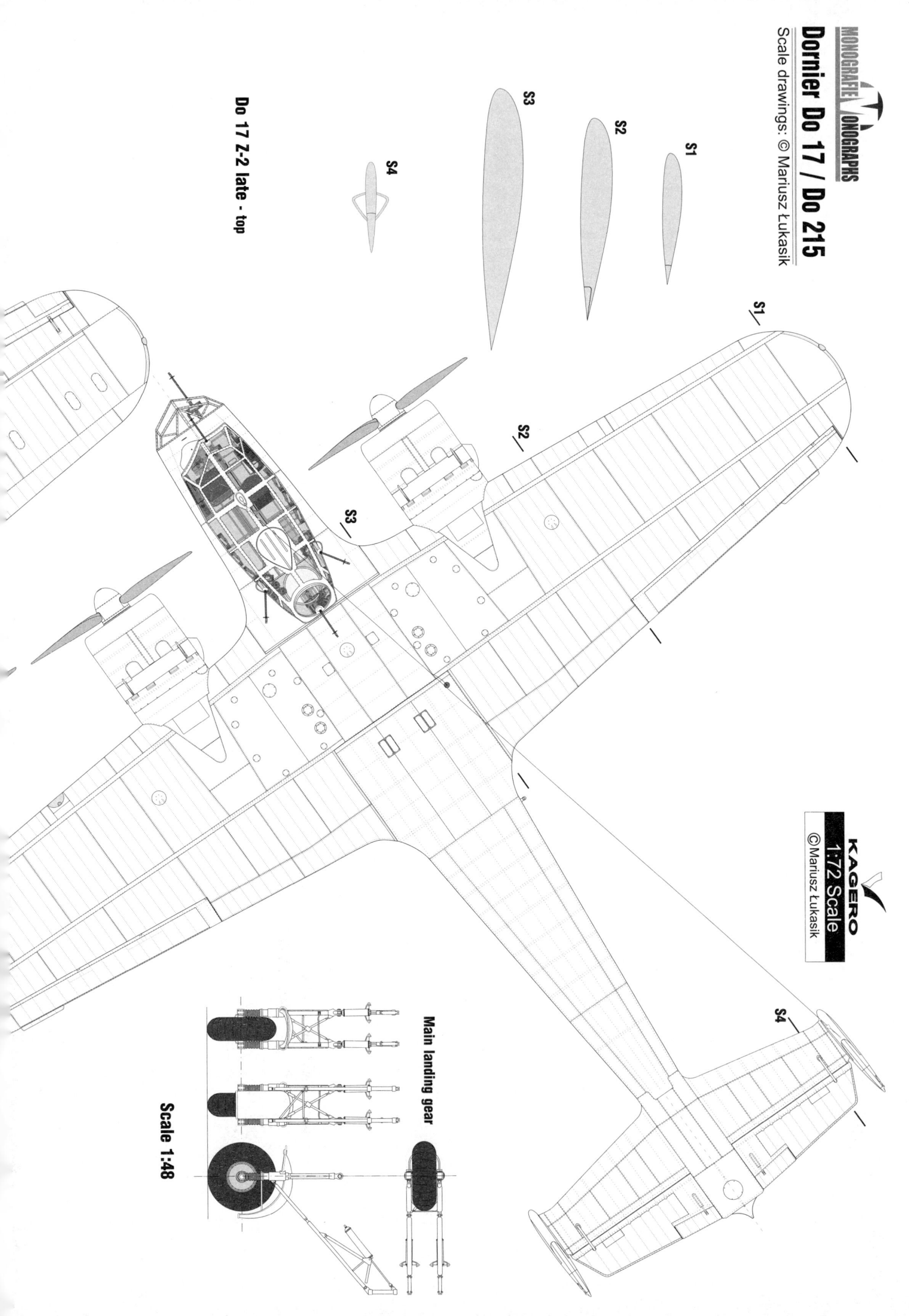

MONOGRAFIE **M**ONOGRAPHS

Dornier Do 17 / Do 215

Scale drawings: © Mariusz Łukasik

Do 17 Z-2 late - top

S1
S2
S3
S4

KAGERO
1:72 Scale
© Mariusz Łukasik

Main landing gear

Scale 1:48

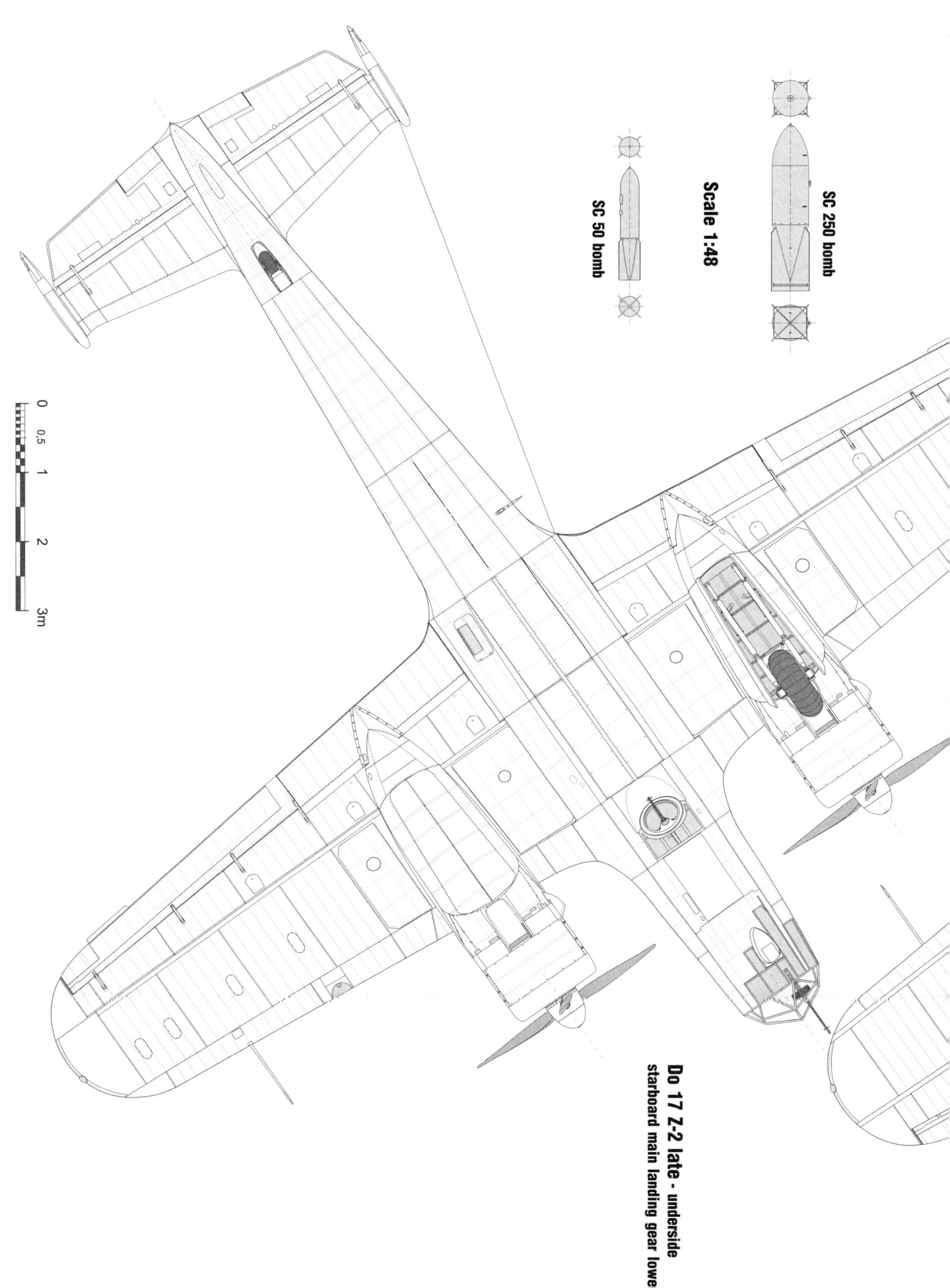

SC 250 bomb

Scale 1:48

SC 50 bomb

Do 17 Z-2 late - underside
starboard main landing gear lowered

0 0,5 1 2 3m

Sheet C

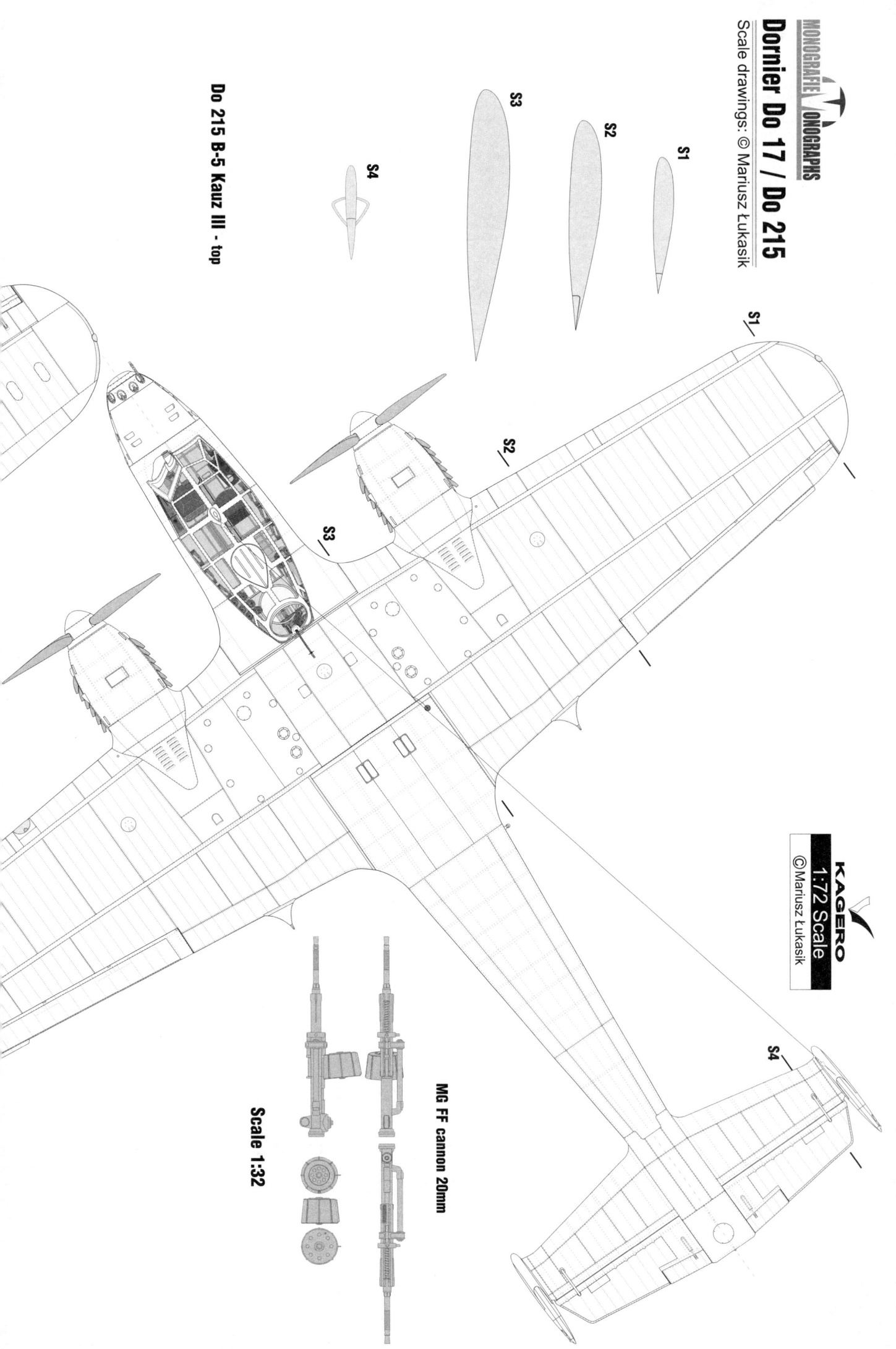

MONOGRAFIE / MONOGRAPHS

Dornier Do 17 / Do 215

Scale drawings: © Mariusz Łukasik

Do 215 B-5 Kauz III - top

S3

S2

S1

S4

S1

S2

S3

S4

KAGERO

1:72 Scale

© Mariusz Łukasik

MG FF cannon 20mm

Scale 1:32

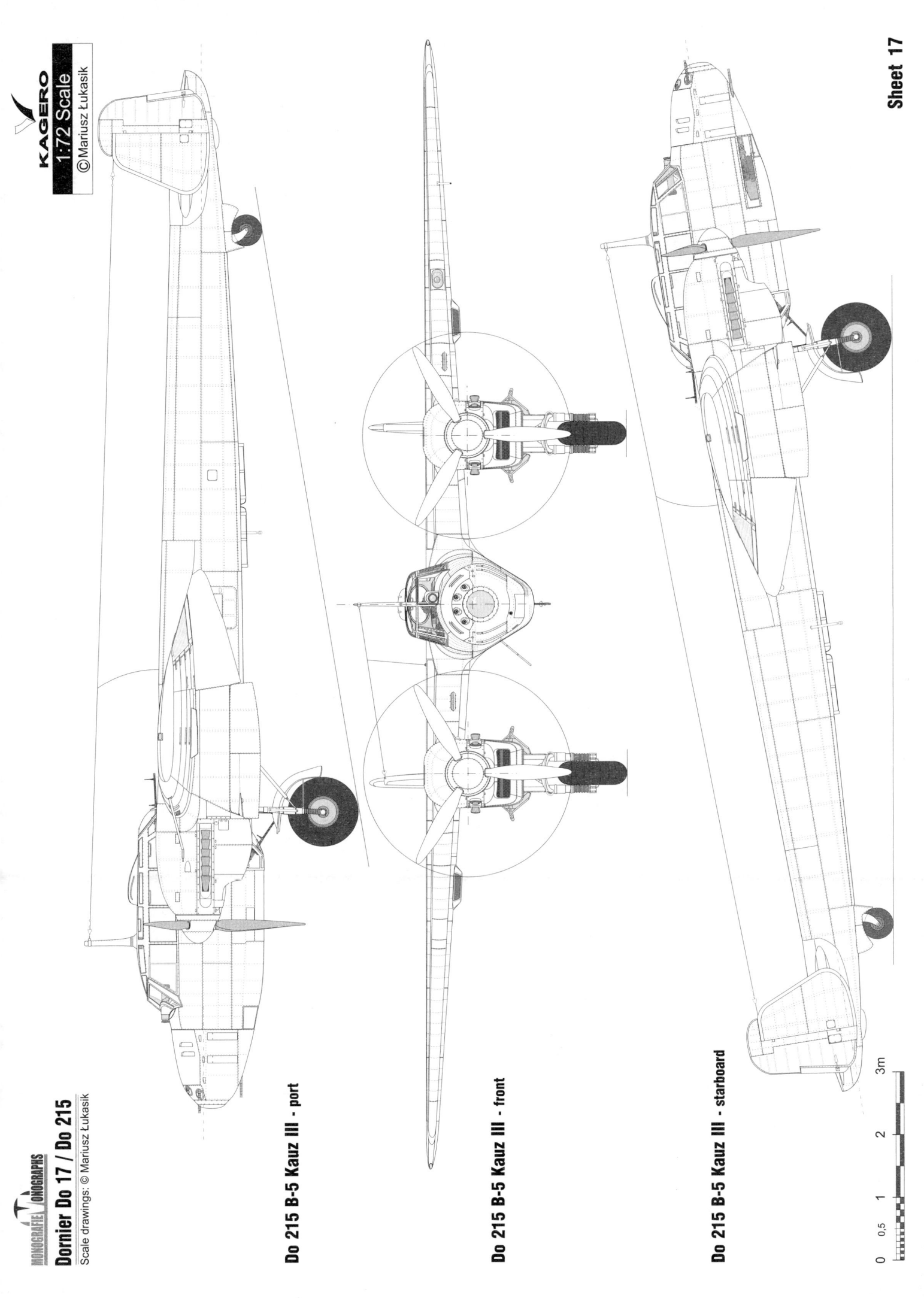

KAGERO

MONOGRAFIE MONOGRAPHS
Dornier Do 17 / Do 215
Scale drawings: © Mariusz Łukasik

1:72 Scale
© Mariusz Łukasik

Sheet 17

Do 215 B-5 Kauz III - port

Do 215 B-5 Kauz III - front

Do 215 B-5 Kauz III - starboard

0   0,5   1   2   3m

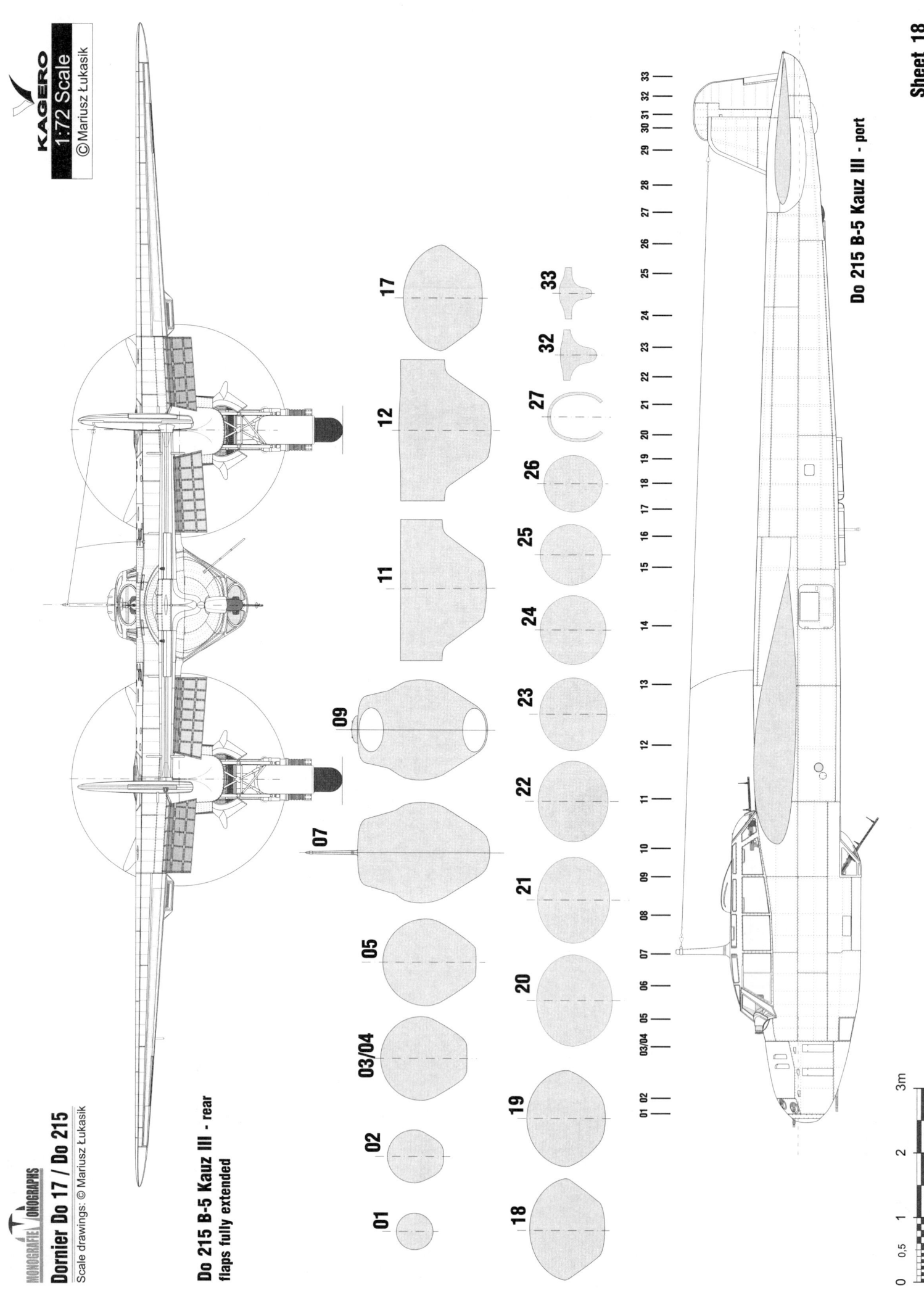

MONOGRAFIE / MONOGRAPHS
Dornier Do 17 / Do 215
Scale drawings: © Mariusz Łukasik

KAGERO
1:72 Scale
© Mariusz Łukasik

Do 215 B-5 Kauz III - rear
flaps fully extended

Do 215 B-5 Kauz III - port

Sheet 18

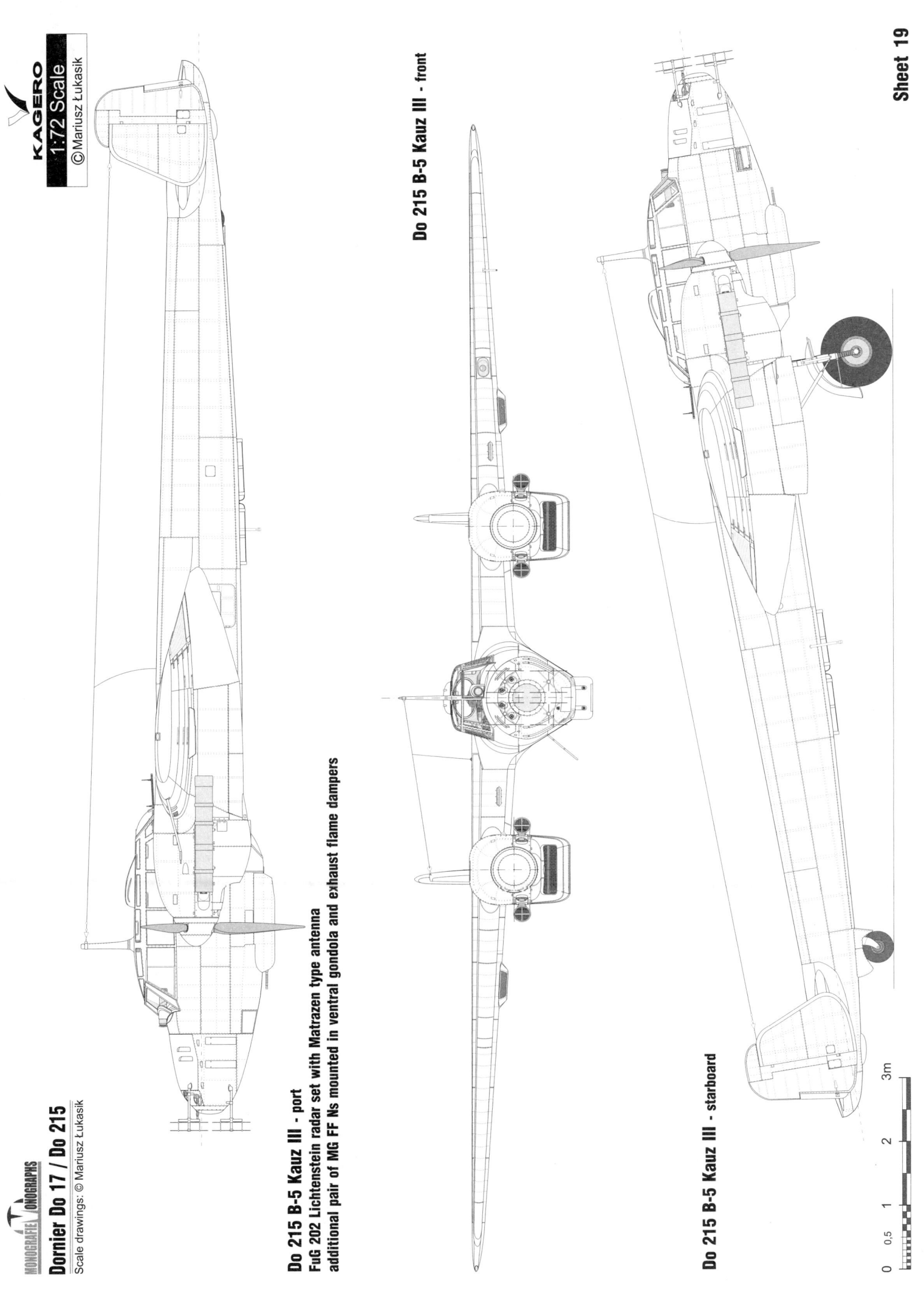

MONOGRAFIE / MONOGRAPHS

Dornier Do 17 / Do 215

Scale drawings: © Mariusz Łukasik

KAGERO

1:72 Scale

© Mariusz Łukasik

Do 215 B-5 Kauz III - port

FuG 202 Lichtenstein radar set with Matrazen type antenna
additional pair of MG FF Ns mounted in ventral gondola and exhaust flame dampers

Do 215 B-5 Kauz III - front

Do 215 B-5 Kauz III - starboard

Sheet 19

0   0,5   1   2   3m

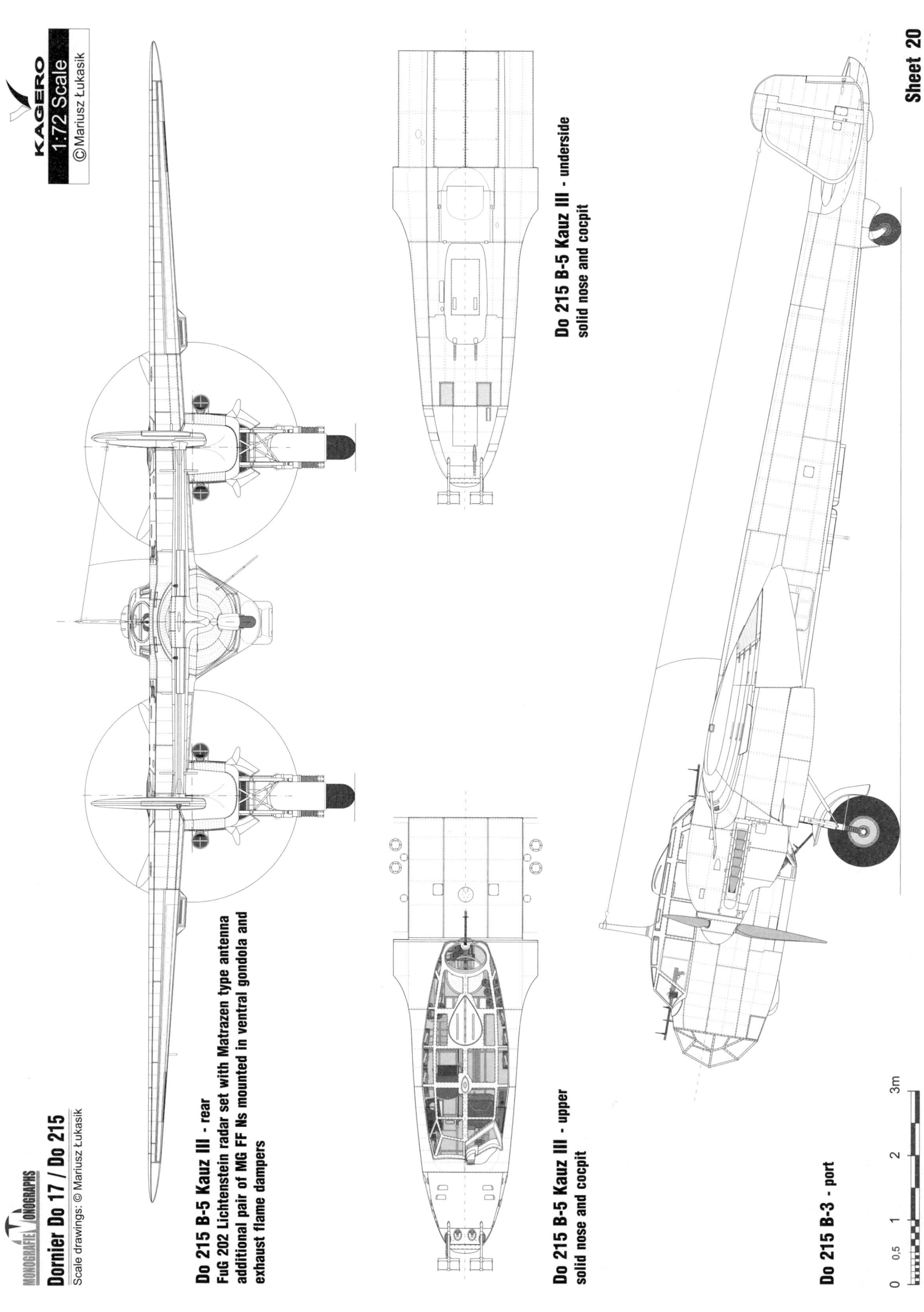

MONOGRAFIE / MONOGRAPHS

Dornier Do 17 / Do 215

Scale drawings: © Mariusz Łukasik

Do 215 B-5 Kauz III - rear
FuG 202 Lichtenstein radar set with Matrazen type antenna
additional pair of MG FF Ns mounted in ventral gondola and
exhaust flame dampers

Do 215 B-5 Kauz III - underside
solid nose and cocpit

Do 215 B-5 Kauz III - upper
solid nose and cocpit

Do 215 B-3 - port

0   0,5   1   2   3m

Specification of external changes

MONOGRAFIE MONOGRAPHS
Dornier Do 17 / Do 215
Scale drawings: © Mariusz Łukasik

KAGERO
1:96 Scale
© Mariusz Łukasik

Dornier Do 17 E-0

Dornier Do 17 E-1

Pitot's tube relocated from mast above cockpit to port wing
Rudder actuator system modified
Two additional MG 15s mounted in front and ventral stations

Dornier Do 17 F

One Rb 10/18, Rb 20/30, and Rb 50/30 cameras apiece mounted in bomb bay;
one hand-held camera
Auxiliary fuel tank mounted in front bay
Bombsight removed

Dornier Do 17 Ka-1

Based on Do 17 E airframe
Powered by Gnome & Rhone 14K engines
MG 15s replaced by Belgian Bauart (Browning) FNs
Fuselage front section lengthened, glazing reduced

changes

Sheet 21

0   0.5   1   2   3m

Specification of external changes

KAGERO
1:96 Scale
© Mariusz Łukasik 2008

Dornier Do 17 M

Powered by Bramo 323 A-1 radials
Engine nacelles modified
New main landing gear wheels and tailwheel
New tailwheel retraction system
3.60 m VDM propeller
Duraplat skinning covers entire airframe
New, electrically-operated split flaps
Fuel tank capacity increased
Elevators' actuator system modified
Cockpit front section modified
Dorsal gun station modified

Dornier Do 17 Kb-2

Based on Do 17 M airframe
Powered by Gnome & Rhone 14K engines
MG 15s replaced by Belgian Bauart (Browning) FNs
Fuselage front section lengthened, glazing reduced

Dornier Do 17 P

Powered by BMW 132 N engines
3.70 m VDM propeller
One Rb 10/18, Rb 20/30, and Rb 50/30 cameras apiece mounted in bomb bay,
besides a hand-held camera
Auxiliary fuel tank mounted in front bay
Bombsight removed

Dornier Do 17 P Nachtaufklärer

ETC 50/VIIIc bomb rack to four LC 50F flare bombs
Camera Rb 50/30 in first bomb bay removed

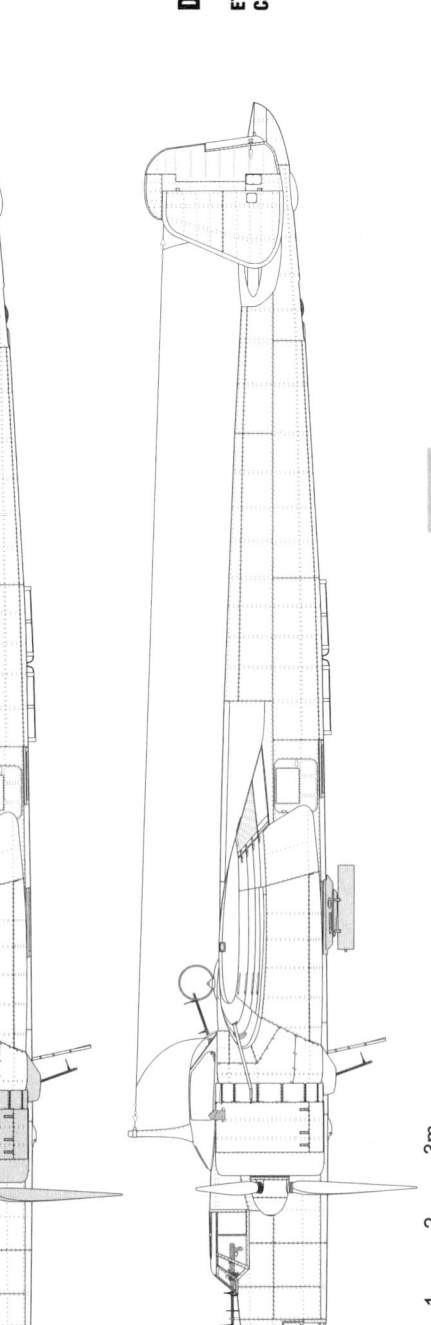

changes

0   0,5   1   2   3m

MONOGRAFIE MONOGRAPHS
Dornier Do 17 / Do 215
Scale drawings: © Mariusz Łukasik

KAGERO
1:96 Scale
© Mariusz Łukasik

Specification of external changes

Dornier Do 17 Z-2

Based on Do 17 M airframe
Powered by Bramo 323 P-1 engines
3.60 m VDM propeller
Fuel tank capacity increased
Fuselage front section and cockpit modified
Three additional MG 15s, in front and side stations
FuG 25 and FuG 10 sets installed
Engine nacelles modified
Cockpit entry hatch relocated to the bottom of fuselage front section
Number of crewmembers increased to four

Dornier Do 17 Z-2 late

Exhaust manifold modified (single exhaust stubs)

Dornier Do 17 Z-3

Rb 20/30 and Rb 50/30 cameras, besides a hand-held camera
MG 15 in ventral stations removed

Dornier Do 17 Z-7 Kauz I

Solid nose, as in Ju 88 C/
Offensive armament of 3 x MG17s and MG FFs or MG 151/20s
Crew reduced to two members
11 mm armoured-glass windshield for pilot

changes

Sheet 23

0   0,5   1   2   3m

KAGERO
1:96 Scale
© Mariusz Łukasik

Specification of external changes

Dornier Do 17 Z-10 Kauz II

Solid, lengthened nose, with Q-Rohr IR searchlight mounted in the nose
Offensive armament increased to 4 x MG 17s and MG FFs or MG 151/20s
Revi C12D sight

Dornier Do 215 B-2

Powered by Daimler Benz DB 601 A-1 engines
3.39 m VDM propeller
Engine nacelles modified
New split flaps

Dornier Do 215 B-4

Rb 20/30 and Rb 50/30 cameras mounted in fuselage front section

Dornier Do 215 B-5 Kauz III

Solid, longer nose (as in Do 17 Z-10 Kauz II)
Some aircraft fitted with FuG 202 Lichtenstein radar set with Matrazen type antenna
Some aircraft armed with additional pair of MG FF Ns mounted in ventral gondola
Exhaust flame dampers

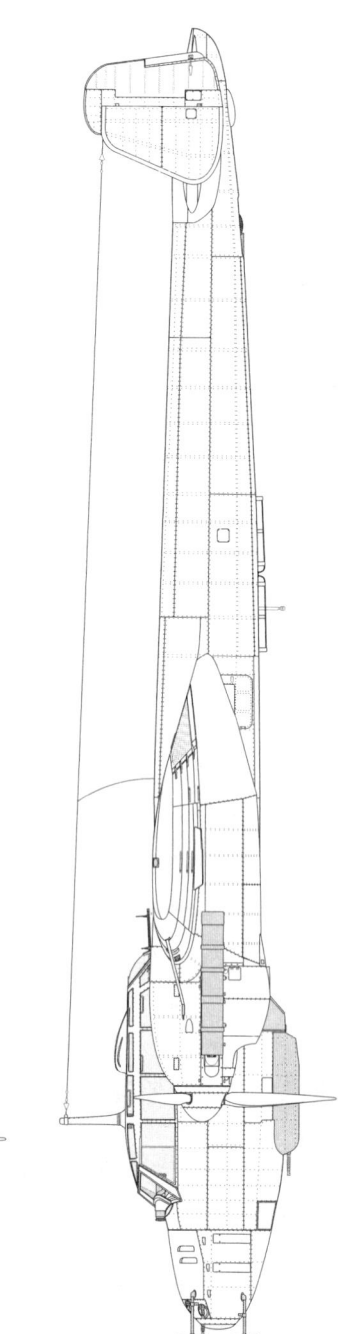

changes

Sheet 24

0   0.5   1   2   3m

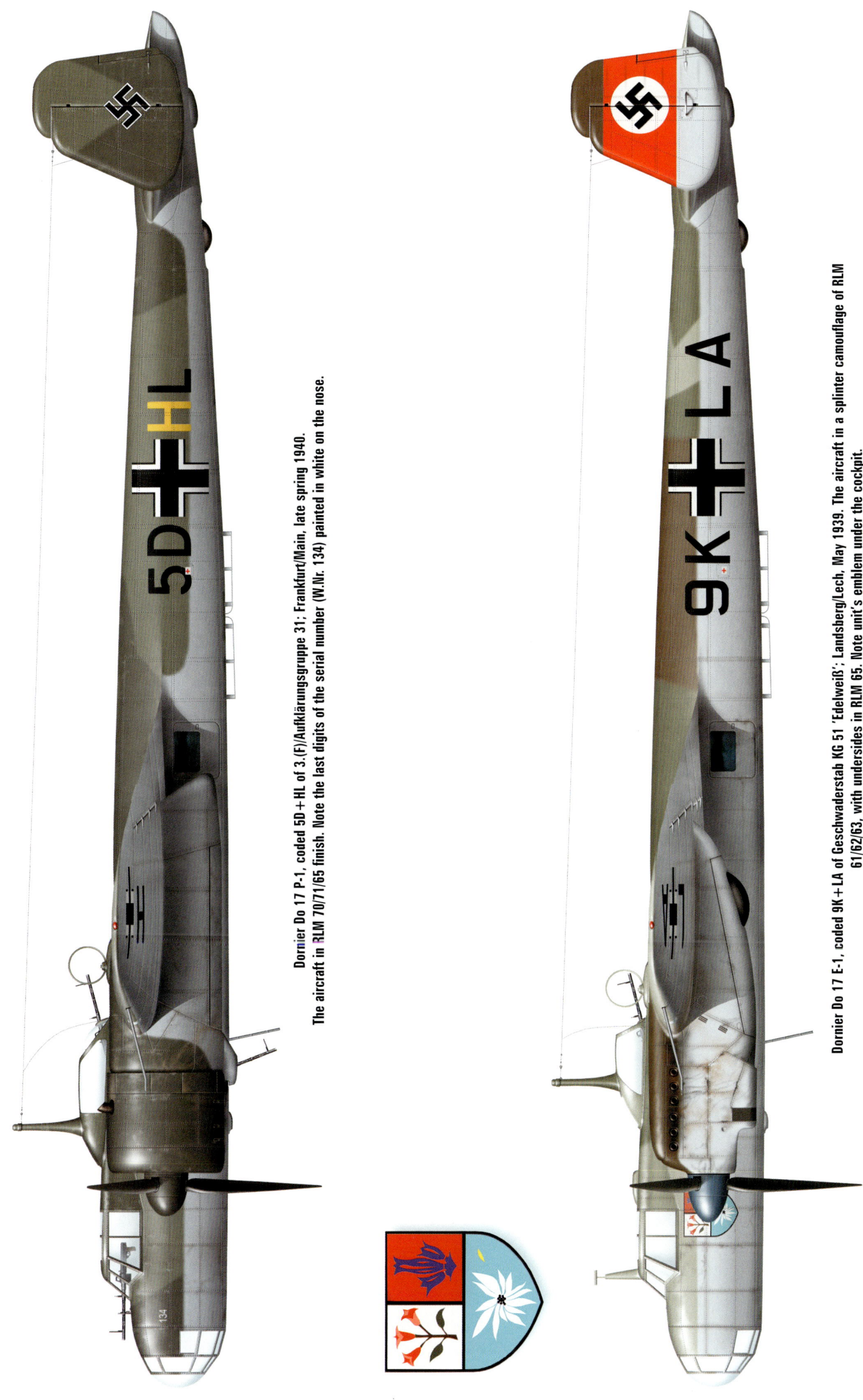

Painted by Arkadiusz Wróbel

Dornier Do 17 P-1, coded 5D+HL of 3.(F)/Aufklärungsgruppe 31; Frankfurt/Main, late spring 1940.
The aircraft in RLM 70/71/65 finish. Note the last digits of the serial number (W.Nr. 134) painted in white on the nose.

Dornier Do 17 E-1, coded 9K+LA of Geschwaderstab KG 51 'Edelweiß'; Landsberg/Lech, May 1939. The aircraft in a splinter camouflage of RLM 61/62/63, with undersides in RLM 65. Note unit's emblem under the cockpit.

Painted by Arkadiusz Wróbel

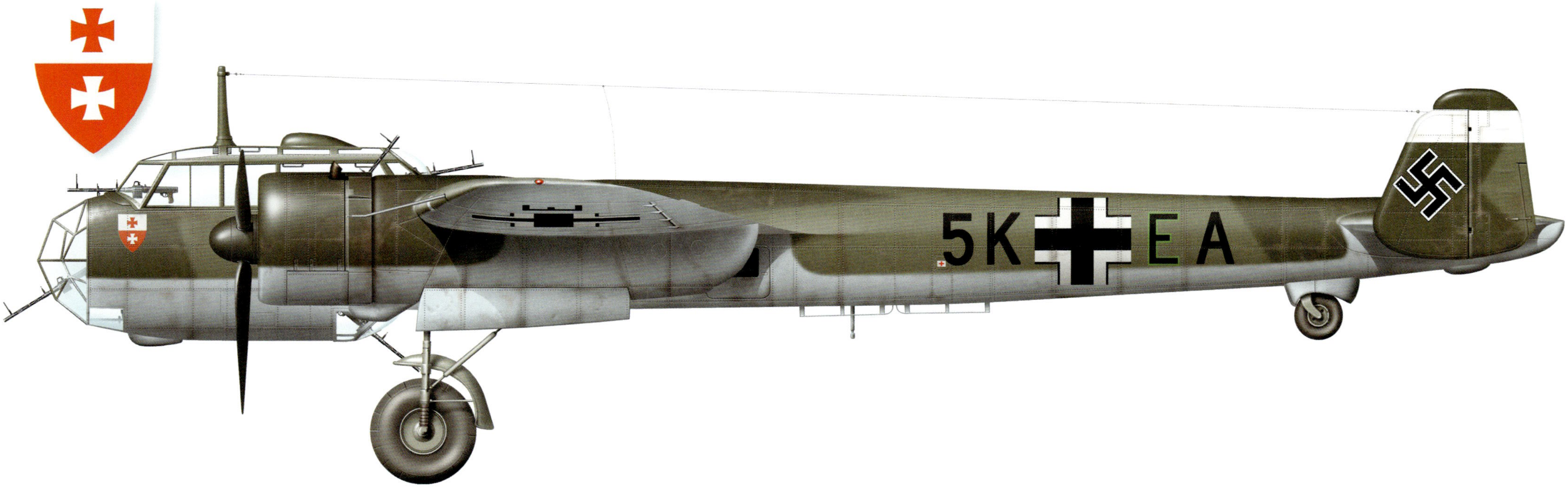

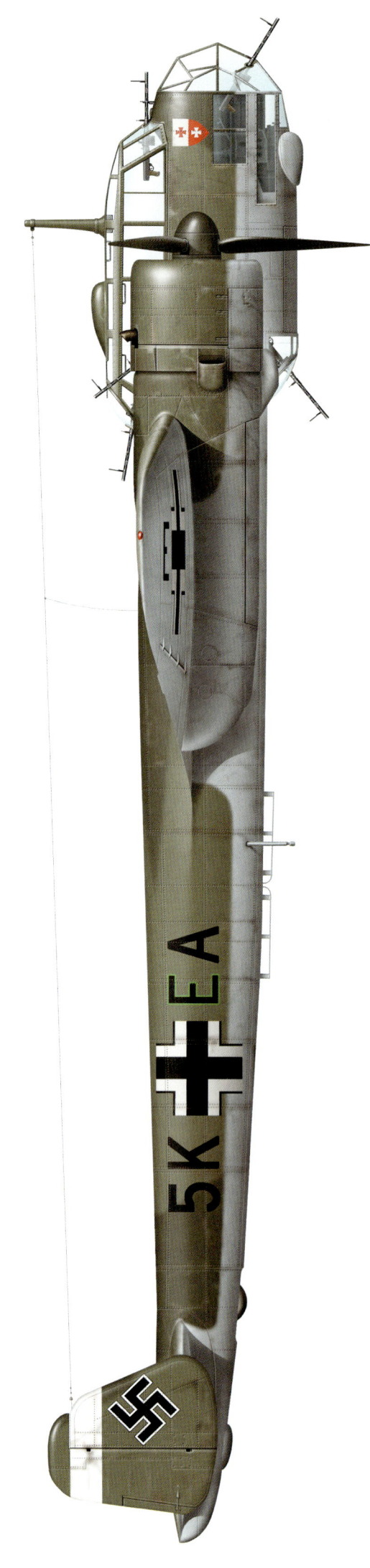

Dornier Do 17 Z-3, coded 5K+EA of Geschwaderstab KG 3 'Blitz'; Le Culot, France, August 1940. The aircraft is finished in RLM 70/71/65.

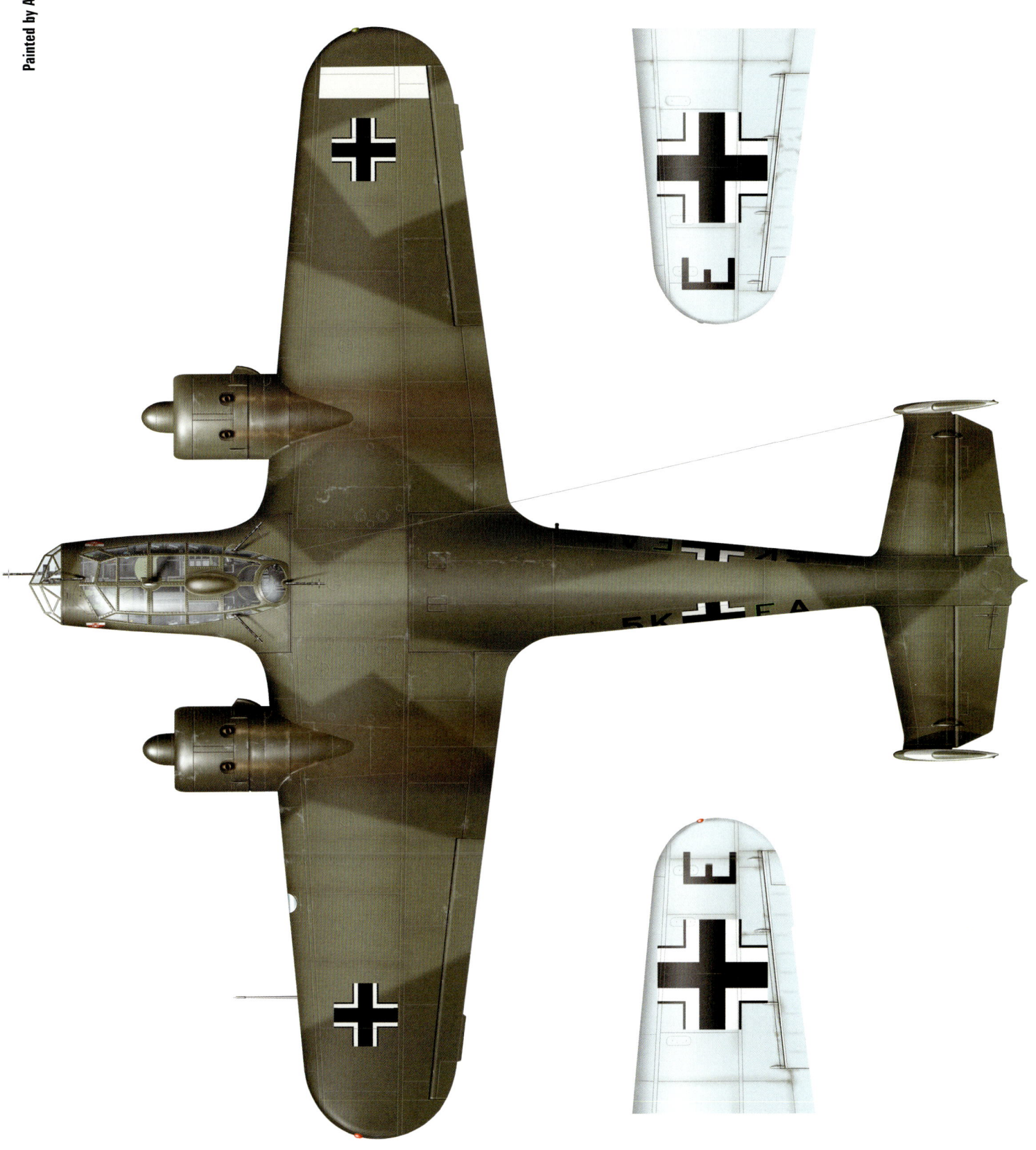

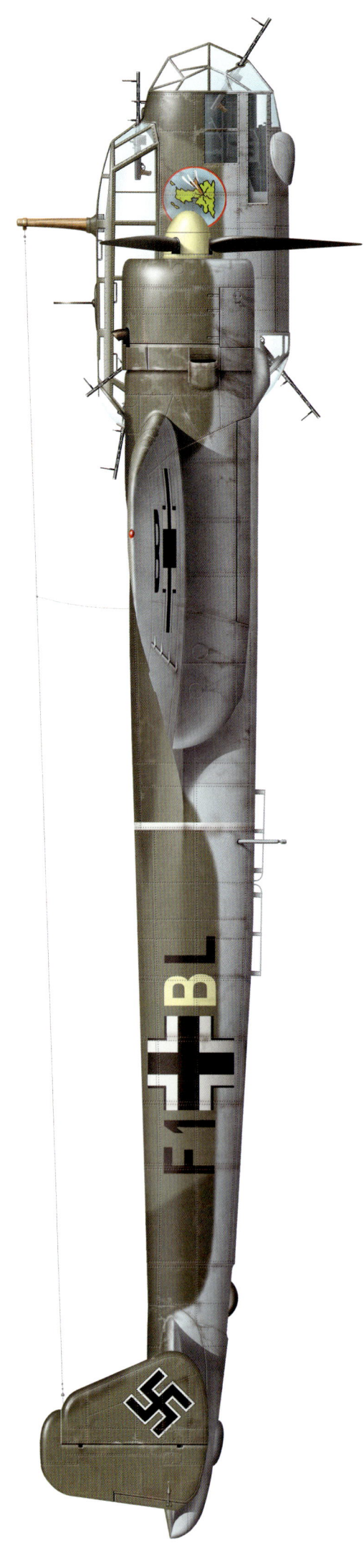

Painted by Arkadiusz Wróbel

Dornier Do 17 Z coded 'F1+BL' of 3./KG 76, 1940. The aircraft is finished in RLM 70/71 on upper surfaces, and RLM 65 on the undersides. Of interest are the little-known emblem of the unit, which was carried on either side of the forward fuselage below the cockpit, and a narrow white band around the fuselage, aft of the wings.

Painted by Arkadiusz Wróbel

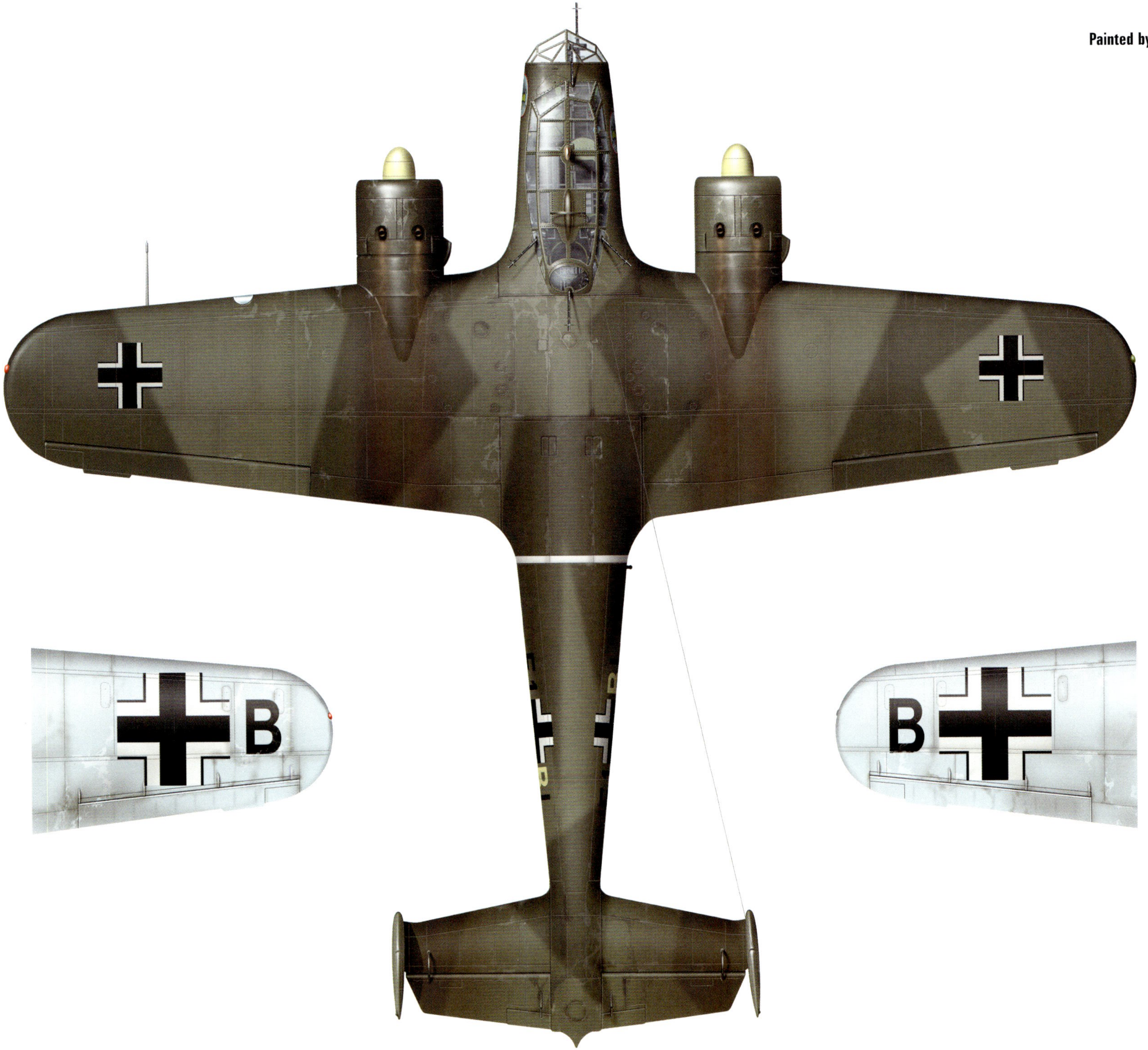

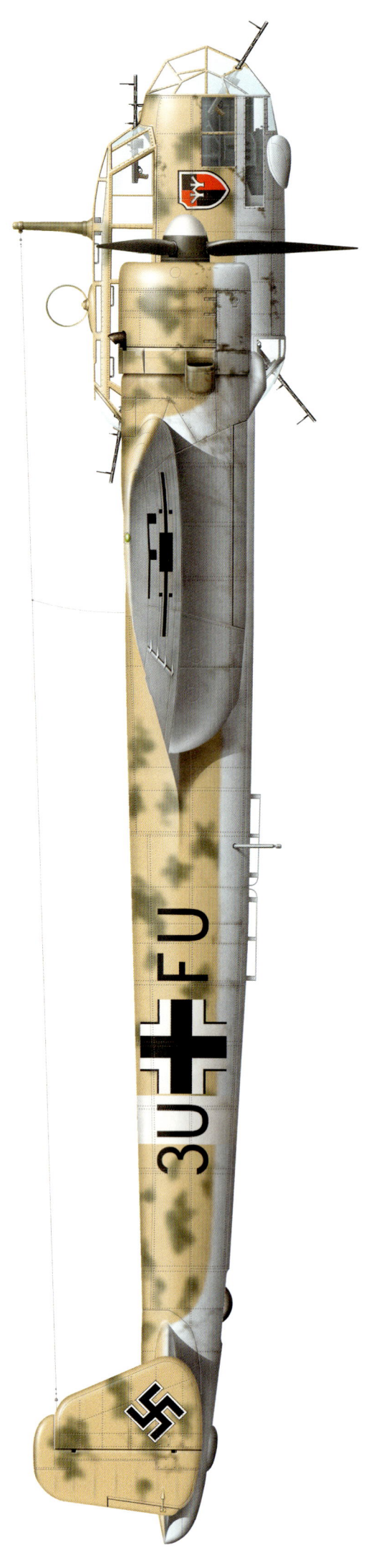

Painted by Arkadiusz Wróbel

Dornier Do 17 Z-1, coded 3U+FU, of 10./ZG 26 'Horst Wessel'; Western Desert, Libya, autumn 1941. The aircraft in tropical RLM 78/79/80 finish, with Geschwader's emblem painted under the cockpit.

Painted by Arkadiusz Wróbel

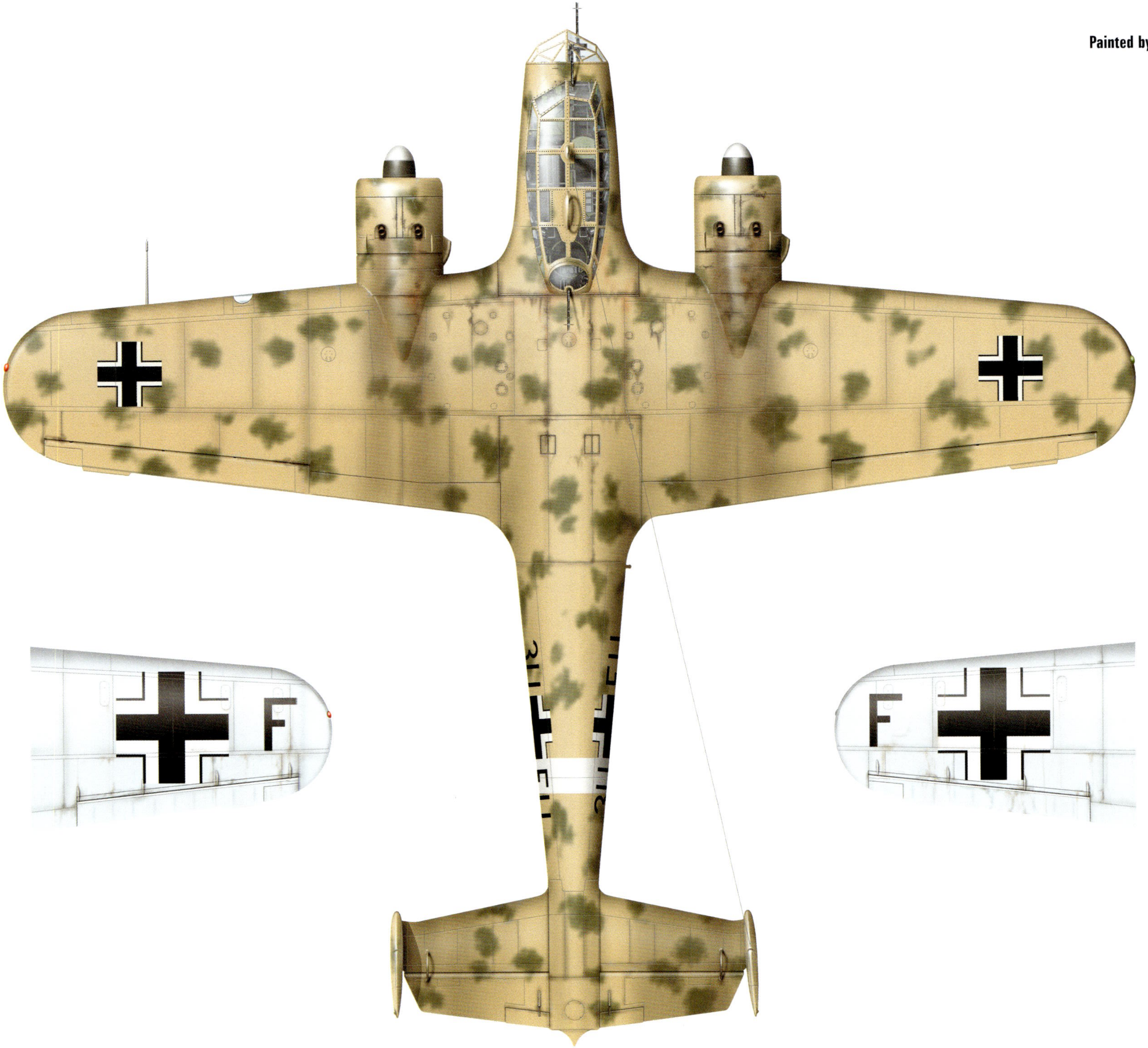

Painted by Arkadiusz Wróbel

Dornier Do 17 Z-2, 5K+FD, Stab der III./KG 3 'Blitz', Heiligenbeil, Eastern Prussia, September 1939. The aircraft is finished in RLM 70/71/65.

Dornier Do 17 Z-2, coded 9K+AM, of 4./KG 3 'Blitz', May 1940. Note unit's emblem under the cockpit. The aircraft is finished in RLM 70/71/65.

Dornier Do 17 Z-2, coded F1+HH of 1./KG 76; France, September 1940. Note unit's emblem under the cockpit. The aircraft is finished in RLM 70/71/65.

Dornier Do 17 Z-7, coded R4+HK of I./NJG 2; Gilze-Rijen, the Netherlands, March 1941. The aircraft camouflaged in overall black. Lower engine cowlings in RLM 65, a white band in rear fuselage. Note unit's emblem under the cockpit.

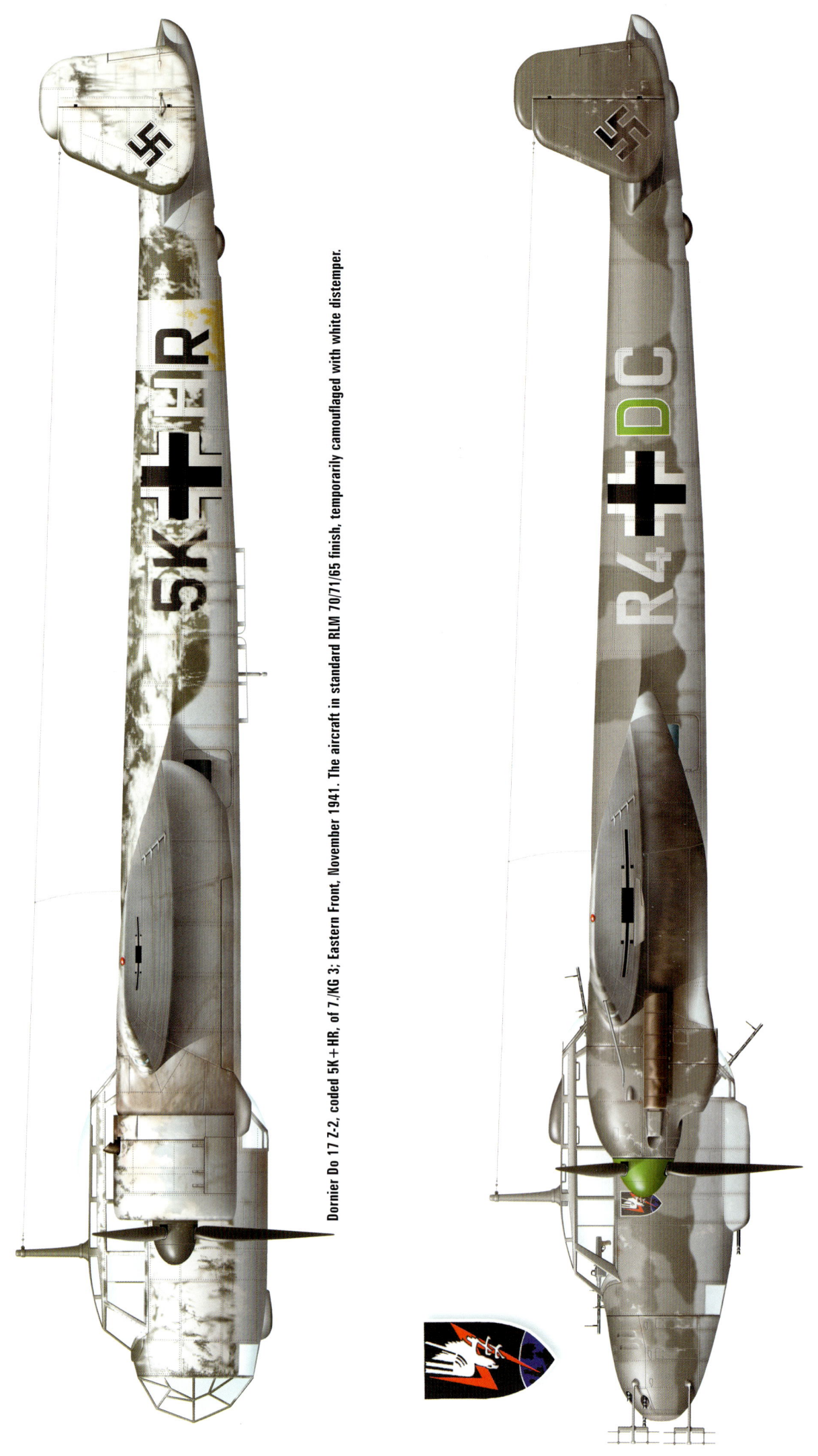

Dornier Do 17 Z-2, coded 5K+HR, of 7./KG 3; Eastern Front, November 1941. The aircraft in standard RLM 70/71/65 finish, temporarily camouflaged with white distemper.

Dornier Do 215 B-5, coded R4+DC of Stab der II./NJG 2; Leeuwarden, the Netherlands, spring 1942. The aircraft camouflaged in RLM 74/75/76, with unit's emblem under the cockpit.